MEĐUGORJE TODAY

MEDJUGORJE

TODAY

Photography by

Tomislav Rastić
Zlata Vucelić
Tomaž Lauko
Jelenko Rastić

Leonard Oreč
Dubravko Horvatić
Ljudevit Rupčić
Slavko Barbarić
René Laurentin
Živko Kustić
Archbishop Frane Franić
Jakov Bubalo
Svetozar Kraljević
Georg W. Kosicki
Mark Miravalle
Vesna Krmpotić

CONTENTS

Dr Leonard Oreč, OFM

THROUGH THE EYE, THE HEART AND REASON

This book is both unusual and simple – and in this it mirrors Medjugor-je. We are left at the end with the impression that we have met the seers; as though one has been to Medjugorje during a period of hiatus and when there is no press of the usual milling crowd of pilgrims; when believers and curious alike are not thronging about the place of Appa-rition; when nothing seemed to happen but where, in fact, everything wears the tangible and ineradicable aura of the events. Eight years have passed since the first excitement was felt by the news of the Apparitions of Our Lady. Surely sufficient time for the phenomenon to have formed its roots and to have matured, not only within the seers and pilgrims themselves but also throughout the whole of the surrounding region. This book is primarily a showcase of artistic photography and a portrait of the daily life of Medjugorje. It is abundandtly clear that the master photographer feels as much with his camera as he does with his heart, and that he has directed his lens towards what he felt to be the radiating source of truth about the people of Medjugorje and the wider popula-tion of Herzegovina. And about God who is recognizably omnispre-sent, in a Herzegovian way. It is almost as if Medjugorje and its Appa-ritions simply had to happen, in order that we could finally see this region in its true colours and these people on their journey through space and time. Just as the Evangelists were able to fully perceive only through the light of the Resurrection and were able to correlate into a single Paschal mystery happening the ordinary events in the life of Jesus – from the light of the Nativity in Bethlehem to the darkness that was Golgotha – so has the artist-photographer exposed afresh many minia-ture cameos of Medjugorje and the land around it in the new light of the Apparitions of Our Lady. In every one of these photographs and in their progression there shines the connecting thread of this new light.

We are, of course, unable to see Our Lady in any of these pictures. There are no photographic "jottings" of the publicized miracles with the sun, with the cross at Križevac; there are no bursts of incandescence or messages written in the sky. What we are able to see, however, are apparently unremarkable landscapes and homely faces; fields dry and greening; a countryside emanating an almost human warmth inconsistent with its barren appearance; shades of evening filled with family prayers spoken around tables and in front of hearths. These are a people, men and women, who at first glance appear to walk with a calm resignation, who are slow of movement, as if in a state of forlorn indolence. But one is able to discern that in their movements, and particularly in their eyes, they carry with them the constant expectation of a miracle. A miracle not as some sensation but rather as the positive intervention of a beneficent God in an otherwise desolate destiny. The stone throws out sparks; eyes radiate with the warmth of hope, a hope born not of naivety but as a feature of human maturity imbued by faith. It is into this ambience that the many pilgrims come, to absorb and immediately radiate it. It is carried by the local Franciscans to inspire as a light of conversion other priests who travel here. This is not a question of some mysterious magnetism emanating from the earth and underground waters, but of centuries of suffering by the believers; in this region the people have firmly tied the knots of hope without which survival would have been impossible. When the kindly reader turns these pages of photographs and sees with a caressing eye, he will understand without need of explanation or convincing that Our Lady not only could but just had to appear somewhere around here. For the people of these parts have, since time beyond remembering, epitomized the suffering at Golgotha and Mary's suffering at the foot of the cross. ■

June 25, 1988

Dear children! Today I am calling you to the love which is loyal and pleasing to God. Little children, love bears everything bitter and difficult for the sake of Jesus who is love. Therefore, dear children, pray God to come to your aid, not, however, according to your desires but according to His love. Surrender yourselves to God so that He may heal you, console you, and forgive everything inside you which is a hindrance on the way of love. In this way God can mould your life and you will grow in love. Dear children, glorify god with the canticle of love so that God's love may be able to grow in you day by day to its fullness. Thank you for having responded to my call.

Tomislav Rastić
Tomaž Lauko    Dubravko Horvatić

THERE, WHERE OUR LADY SPEAKS CROATIAN

Between the chain of Dalmatian mountains in the west – which still further west plunge headlong into the sea – and the turbulent Neretva river in the east that has carved ravines and gorges as well as creating fertile valleys, lies western Herzegovina. Its northern boundary is a bulwark of mountains (Čabula, Čvrsnica, Lipa and Vran) and the wide Duvno plains (Duvanjsko Polje); to the east, again the Neretva – now in its lower reaches – and the Dalmatian mountains. It is generally thought that Herzegovina is barren and ruggedly rockbound; it is true that the terrain is mostly sterile and uninviting karst, but extremely fertile areas do exist also. The most productive of such areas in the whole of Herzegovina is undoubtedly Brotnjo, that part of the country around Medjugorje to the south of western Herzegovina. It is from the location of these rich and bountiful lands that the name of the area derives (medju gorje – between the mountains) and there is a history of continuous human settlement hereabouts from prehistoric times. Although no traces of Stone Age man have been found in Brotnjo (contrary to some other parts of Herzegovina, on both sides of the Neretva river) finds have been unearthed there which date from the Bronze Age, particularly its later periods.

In the Iron Age Brotnjo was peopled by the Illyrian tribes of Ardi-jejan, Autarijati and Daorsan. Today's still visible signs of their presence here take the form of hill-forts and remains of fortified settlements on elevated sites. Necropoles of these hill-forts have revealed to archaeologists a wealth of Illyrian tools and weapons, jewellery and vessels. In Bijakovići, on the Crnica mountain, where the seers live, stands an Illyrian hill-fort, not far distant from where the first encounters with Our Lady occurred. The Illyrian domination over Brotnjo is also evidenced by their tumuli – graves that are covered by mounds consisting of great numbers of stones. These now bramble-stitched tumuli stand out from the landscape of Brotnjo like huge hemispheres. They are for the most part still unresearched and we are not privy to the secrets they guard about the aborigines of this region. The Celts, who arrived in these parts towards the end of the fourth and the beginning of the third century BC, are even more shadowy figures since material traces of their culture are yet more scarce. There are, however, vestiges which indicate points of contact between them, the Illyrians and the Hellenes, particularly with the latter, who colonized the islands of Vis and Hvar: specifically, Greek coins have been found at several locations in Brotnjo and in Medjugorje generally. On the other hand, evidence of Roman presence abounds. They began their incursions into these parts after 229 BC following their victory over the Illyrian tribes. The stelae of Roman soldiers that were found in Brotnjo are kept in the Regional Museum in Sarajevo and in the Museum of the Franciscan Monastery (founded 1884) at Humac, near Ljubuški. It is evident from some of those tombstones that the castrum at Bigeste included a stomenason's workshop. This large military encampment, remains of which have been preserved, was situated at Gračine, near Humac on the left bank of the Trebižat river and on an important road linking Salona (today's Solin, near Split) with Narona (today, the village of Vid on the Neretva river, where there are houses built entirely from elements of Roman monuments). In Brotnjo it is possible to see the remains of several basilicas dating from the late Antique period and it is likely that there was a Roman basilica in Medjugorje, in the Srebrenica locality. In front of the church in nearby Čerin there is a small collection of stone fagments and monuments: an altar of Silvanus and Diana, a relief depicting figures of a horseman and a chained female slave, a milestone, a late Antique sarcophagus bearing a cross, and an olive press. Oh, yes! In the Brotnjo of those times there were olive groves, but no sign of them remains today. And even more – Roman sources speak to us of forests; they say that the whole of Herzegovina was wooded and that timber was exported as far abroad as Italy. South of Brotnjo, in Mogorjelo (near Čapljina), shaded and shielded by cypress trees stand the preserved remains of a large Roman estate (villa rustica). During the course of the upheavals caused by the great migration of peoples it was repeatedly destroyed and rebuilt, to be finally razed by the Goths in the fifth century. However, by as early as the first half of the sixth century Byzant became the dominant power, establishing its rule not only in Herzegovina but also throughout the entire Balkan area. The numismatic collection of the museum in Humac contains a considerable number of early Byzantine coins that were found around Brotnjo.

The Croats, who today comprise 99% of the population of western Herzegovina – and therefore of Brotnjo – came to these parts in the third decade of the seventh century at the invitation of Heracles, the Byzantine Emperor, who enlisted their aid in his fight against the Avars and Slavic tribes who were threatening the Empire. The Croats were to create their own strong State on the coast of the Adriatic Sea and in its hinterland, a State which on 21 June 879 during the reign of Prince Branimir was recognized near and far as an independent and sovereign State. Forty kilometres to the north of Medjugorje we find the extensive Duvno plains (Duvanjsko polje) where, as tradition has it, the first King of Croatia was crowned. At that time Brotnjo belonged to the district of Hum or Zahumlje which, as an autonomous area, was within the Croatian State. Mihajlo Višević, the Prince of Hum, together with King Tomislav, confirmed the resolutions made by the State Assembly held in Split in 925, where the question of Church jurisdiction in Croatia was discussed.

The majority of Croats adopted Christianity around the middle of the seventh century (the Museum of Croatian Archaeology in Split contains the baptistry of Prince Višeslav from the ninth century). From that period churches were built throughout Croatian lands in a style now known as early Croatian. Many of the churches that were built between the ninth and twelfth centuries have been preserved, to be seen mainly along the Croatian Adriatic coast. Churches in the hinterland were to suffer destruction in wars and in their aftermath by the conquerors of the day; as a consequence not a single preserved church from that period exists today in Brotnjo. It is an unarguable fact, however, that somewhere around Humac in the tenth/eleventh century there stood the church of St Michael the Archangel, built by Uskrsimir, son of Bret and his wife Pavica. This is testified to by the Plaque of Humac dating from that period – which in itself is of considerable importance, being as it is one of the oldest monuments bearing a Croatian language text – it is certainly the oldest example in Herzegovina. It is written in the Croatian variation of Ćirilica – Bosančica (the Bosnian Ćyrillic script) and includes some letters from the old Croatian Glagoljica script.

Following the deaths of King Tomislav and Prince Mihajlo Višević the whole of what we know today as Herzegovina – and therefore Brotnjo – was from time to time to fall outside the borders of the Croatian State, particularly during the periods of dynastic conflicts and other political upheavals which were to weaken the political and military power of Croatian rulers. When, in 1102, Croatia entered into a personal union with Hungary, the area of Hum was not then under the sway of Croatian rule. It was occasionally to feel the weight of the Croatian-Hungarian King's mace but in the main it was controlled by the small States of Zeta and Raška, depending upon who was the stronger in any given period. From 1322 Hum was to form part of the State of Bosnia, but the real power was held by the Princes of Hum. The best-known of these was Stipan Vukčić Kosača, an independent ruler who in 1448 had the title "Herzeg of St Saba" bestowed upon him by Pope Nicholas V and it is from this time that Hum came to be known as Herzegovina. We can still see his relatively well-preserved fortified towns rising above Blagaj on the Buna river, and above Ljubuški.

From the period between the thirteenth to the beginning of the sixteenth century many examples of standing tombstones (stećci) have been preserved throughout Dalmatia, Herzegovina and Bosnia and which were, just like early Croatian architecture, indigenous to these parts. A stećak is a form of tombstone which can take one of a number of diverse shapes and sizes (sarcophagi, i.e. narrow and slender parallelepipeds; gabled, i.e. a monolith sarcophagus with a ridged top; column and cross-shaped). They are decorated with symbolic ornamentations and floral motifs, with reliefs of waggons, hunting, duelling and similar scenes. Inscribed into these rough and simple but nevertheless monumental and impressive cromlechs, are traces reminiscent not only of the local early Croatian, but also of Romanesque and Gothic forms. It was thought for a long time that this sepulchral art was linked exclusively to the Medieval heretical cult of the Bogomils, which was particularly widespread in Herzegovina and Bosnia, but more recent research has shown that standing tombstones were common to both Catholic and Bogomil. In Brotnjo there is a number of necropoles comprising such tombstones, as indeed there is in the neighborhood of Medjugorje. There are also traces of Medieval churches. The area of Medjugorje probably belonged to the church of St Gregory, which is mentioned in 1307 in Brotnjo, that is, Broćno, as the region was known at that time.

Following the fall of Bosnia to the Turks in 1463, the same fate threatened Herzegovina; Turkish armies were conquering territory in progressive stages and twenty years after Bosnia fell the turn of Herzegovina came. Turkish rule meant the imposition of the faith of Islam and an intolerance towards the infidel population, especially so during the periods of Turkish wars with Christian lands. It was during such periods that a heightened persecution of Christians was seen; churches were either burned or totally destroyed, or they were converted into mosques. The parish of Medjugorje is first mentioned in 1599 but by the following century it had ceased to exist. The eighteenth century saw the reappearance of Medjugorje within the parish of Brotnjo, which was established in Gradnići, near Čitluk, in 1825. The spiritual leaders of the parish were the Franciscans, who came to Herzegovina at the beginning of the fifteenth century and who shared with their people the four centuries of Turkish tyranny. Since the nature of the work of the Franciscans was mostly clandestine, they left no structures to mark their passing or their pastoral labors; they did, however, leave a deeply entrenched faith in the hearts of the common people. Indeed, they would sometimes celebrate Mass – as was common in the proto-Christian era – in caves, in deep forest, in mountain clearings and in other secluded places, where both they and their people were screened from Turkish eyes. Meanwhile, the Turks were constructing their towers in the villages of Brotnjo; they are to be seen today – some preserved, others in ruin – in other villages in Medjugorje and Bijakovići. In Brotnjo itself signs of Islamic archtecture are almost non-existent since there never has been, nor is there, an Islamic population of any real size.

It was only as a result of the advent of Austro-Hungarian rule in 1878 that the Catholic Church was allowed to practise and propagate its faith throughout Herzegovina without let or hindrance. In 1892 the Franciscans founded a parish in Medjugorje and in 1897 they built the church of St Jacob which, as it had been built on soft and porous ground, had to be replaced by a new one a mere forty years later. Designed by the Zagreb architect Stjepan Podhorski (who had already designed several churches based on the model of early Croatian architecture), its construction began in 1937. However, the Second World War halted all work and its resumption was further delayed due to the poverty of post-war years. The church – whose name today has spread around the world – was finally completed in 1969 and became the Parish Church of Medjugorje, Bijakovići, Miletino, Vionica and Šurmanci. Sadly, the original concept of the architect Podhorski was completely altered during the course of constructon and consequently, within and without, the building bears no characteristics which could link it with the traditional sacral architecture of our southern parts, or even with the landscape from which it springs. In the period between the two World Wars Medjugorje was to acquire yet another sacral monument – a 14 metre-high cross was erected on a hill which from then on was to be known as Križevac – to commemorate the 1,933rd anniversary of the birth of Christ and the 1,900th anniversary of His death.

We mentioned earlier that the fields of Brotnjo constitute the most fertile region of Herzegovina. Despite this fact, however, life has never been easy here – neither in the remote past nor in more recent times. Following the end of Turkish oppression in the nineteenth century, particularly in its latter years, there was a massive rise in the birth rate and even these fertile lands were unable to provide for the rapidly growing population. During the First World War Herzegovina was struck by famine. It was then that Fra Didak Buntić (born in Paoča near Čitluk in 1871; died in Čitluk in 1922), already well-known as builder of the magnificent Franciscan basilica on Široki Brijeg, champion of education in Herzegovina and organizer of literacy courses, a man generally recognized as a great benefactor of the people, organized the evacuation of the children of Herzegovina to the northern Croatian regions so that they would not starve to death in their native land. After the end of World War I there began an exodus from Herzegovina to other Croatian lands and abroad, an exodus that continues to this day. (Croats in Bosnia and Herzegovina represent the largest migration coefficient in SFR Yugoslavia). An old saw runs thus: "Herzegovina has peopled all the lands, and still her population stands". In the period between the two great wars emigration was accelerated due to Serbian chauvinistic State policies which manifested themselves in undisguised robbery of the Herzegovian peasantry when buying up their main produce – tobacco and wine. As an example of this, in 1921 the pruchase price of top quality Herzegovian tobacco was 7 dinars per kilogram, but the far poorer-quality Serbian tobacco was being bought by the State for 13.5 dinars. One of the leading human rights campaigners for the people of Herzegovina in the newly created Kingdom of Serbs, Croats and Slovenes (to be named Yugoslavia in 1929) was the previously mentioned Fra Didak Buntić.

In the period 1916-18 the parish of Medjugorje suffered the loss of some 300 souls, and in World War II and in its immediate aftermath a further 350. Both the war and the post-war period dealt merciless blows to the people of western Herzegovina. It took a long time and huge efforts for the wounds of this long-suffering land and its population to heal.

In places the landscape of western Herzegovina appears almost unreal. The fascinating forms of karst country, where a free and imaginative spirit may discern strange images; sky-scraping rocks in the gorges towering above the Neretva river and above other, smaller, meandering rivers; crags rising above broad fields where, come fall, silent waters form and settle, to stay 'til spring (the poet A. B. Šimić says: "I fancy I see... the back of some primeval woman."), since the abysses in the plains cannot absorb all the swollen subterranean rivers rising at the edges of the plains. And then, sometimes, above it all, the naked hills, "this petrified blue eternity" – as the Croatian poet from these parts, Antun Branko Šimić (Drinovci, 1898 – Zagreb, 1925) and mentioned a few lines previously, said. In karstic Herzegovina, within reach of Brotnjo, the small Trebižat river magically transforms itself into the waterfalls of Kočuša and Kravica, oases of green in a desert of karst, two fairy-tales penned by the hand of nature; particularly beautiful is Kravica. This semicircular fall measures about 120 metres wide and 25 metres high. All around is greenery of all descriptions, and in abundance – bushes, shrubs, tussocks of grass, the slender shapes of the poplars soaring above the mills ... Brotnjo itself is a karstic plateau with tablelands and depressions, vast areas of stone and thorn bush, a landscape which seems to belong to some other planet; but there are also numerous fields of fertile red or sandy soil. In these fields the precious ears of wheat, barely and rye form; strips of tobacco plants, their rosy flowers prominent against green leaf. With the arrival of autumn those broad tobacco leaves are hung out to dry, threaded on strings between poles and hooks in front of and on the houses of the Herzegovian peasants, until they turn golden. Tobacco and wine is the main produce of Herzegovian agriculture. Vineyards extend through the fields and down the hillsides; the wine grown in the fields is the dark, ruby red Blatina, while from the grapes on the hills comes the liquid gold of Žilavka. It is from the marc of this fruit that pure grape brandy is produced. Žilavka has been grown here since Roman times and mention was made of it in the Čitluk Charter of 1353 issued by the Ban (Viceroy) Tvrtko. It is considered that the finest Žilavka is produced in the villages of Vionica and Paoče, as the vineyard slopes there ensure the best exposure to the sun. And the quality of Brotnjan tobacco is certainly accounted for by the Mediterranean climate. The warm winds, which from the sea are channelled to these parts through the Neretva valley, bring with them a climate similar to the Mediterranean – mild with many sun – filled days and few that are cloudy or rainy. Fruit and vegetables ripen early here, as much as a month or two before those in other continental regions, and this is one of the greatest of gifts to the agricultural economy. In addition to cherries sweet and sour, peaches and other continental fruit that is grown here are also Mediterranean fruits such as almonds, pomegranates, figs and others. In the groves and woods and side by side with oak, maple, hornbeam and ash are pine, spruce, cypress, etc. The woods give cover and shelter to game big and small (hare, marten, fox, wolf and bear); the rivers teem with fish, with trout predominating. Partridges nest in the rocky hills where the groves and caves are full of wild pigeons and the fields are full of pheasants. The heady scents of sage and thyme, of heather, imortelle and other medicinal and honey-giving herbs permeate through the whole area. Numerous beehives indicate that apiculture is a highly developed industry; the herbs that are drying everywhere underline the fact that the best-known folk doctors come from Herzegovina. These aromatic herbs impart their own very specific flavors to lamb and to ewe's milk cheese. The breeding of sheep is well developed but other livestock is also kept, including goats, cattle and horses. In high summer, when the heat becomes oppressive and drought is prevalent, the sheep are herded to the pastures of Čabulja, Čvrsnica, Vran, Ljubuša and of other mountains. The shepherds, known as planištars, remain with their flocks from the beginning of June until the end of September. They make cheese which they store in the skins of lambs and sheep, to be enjoyed during the winter time and to be washed down with the dark-red Blatina or golden Žilavka. For centuries it was the practise for the shepherds to be accompanied by a Friar who acted as their spiritual guide. And even today, each Sunday, the Franciscans go to the mountains to celebrate Mass with the shepherds. An altar is erected not far from lake Blidi, between Čvrsnica and Vrana not far from the standing tombstones which are scattered around the countryside. It was in this region, at the beginning of the seventeenth century, that Mijat Tomić, outlaw and fighter against the Turkish tyranny and whose name is often eulogized in Croatian folk songs, "held court". The onset of autumn sees the return of the shepherds from the virginal mountain regions to their straggling villages strung out along the edges of fields or on the mounatin slopes. There are few houses remaining that are examples of the old architecture of these parts – houses constructed from large stone blocks and built in the old dry-wall fashion, where the stones adhere one to the next with no mortar or other binding agent, covered either with straw or stone slabs and encircled by walls built by using the same dry-wall technique. Rising above the villages in which modern houses of standard construction now predominate, are the tall silhouettes of church bell towers – and from afar it appears as though flocks of white sheep are gathered around their shepherds. ■

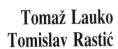

Tomaž Lauko
Tomislav Rastić

Dr Ljudevit Rupčić, OFM

OUR LADY MEETS WITH HER PEOPLE

Our Lady has come to the people, to her children. She has been drawn by her Motherhood and by the trouble in which they find themselves. The timing and manner of her appearance have been dictated by the circumstances in which people today live. It is not only a question of troubles but also of an insidious danger that is neither clearly perceived nor taken seriously; and yet this peril alone is capable of destroying the human species, of placing in jeopardy God's creative plan, of usurping Christ and His work for the salvation of all peoples with the individous aim of replacing Him with perdition. Never before has man been faced by such a spectre and never before has he been less able to defend himself unaided. Having lost control of its destiny mankind has awakened and caused to be arrayed against itself the dormant, destructive forces that exist within man and nature. An obscured sense of morality has favoured the exchange of good for evil. In the transference čof the centre of everything from God to man the balance of the world has shifted from its pivot and the unity of humanity has been atomized, resulting in the destruction of spatial harmony.

Evil in itself constitutes no real danger as long as it is regarded to be evil; whilst it can be seen for what it is there will exist at least the desire for its extirpation. It is only when one begins to see good in evil that its character becomes fell. Neither is impotence destructive, while man is cognizant of it. He will take notice of it if nought else. It only becomes a true destroyer when it is regarded as limitless power. Hunger, *per se*, also poses no threat as long as it is interpreted as a caveat of impending catastrophe. The alarm it causes will motivate people to try to eradicate it. Hunger is deadly when it becomes a feeling of fullness. Again, ignorance is not pernicious as long as it is conscious. Man will attempt to overcome it. The danger lies in beginning to take ignorance for wisdom and when programmes of life are based upon it. It is tragic when, in complete awareness and with presumptuous ignorance and uncontrolled force, retrogression is portrayed as progress and the road to life is diverted to the road of death. General human experience shows with crystal clarity that this is the contemporary reality of life. It is this that has moved Our Lady and caused her to show herself in visible form, to stand before her people and to speak the words of a mother with arms open wide, to prevent the migration of peoples into nullity.

Failed man

Everything indicates that the problems faced by modern man go much deeper than the problems of mere bread, shelter and clothing. Indeed, these factors would not represent problems were it not that there is a far more fundamental cause for unease. The truth of the axiom "...Man is a creature who lives not upon bread alone..." becomes more apparent with each passing day.

It is particularly distressing that many if not all answers have no relevance to the questions posed by contemporary society. The human mind, science and technology necessarily lead – by monopolizing answers to man's questions – to simplification and unilaterality and their absolutization to the inevitable destruction of humanity. Man is imprisoned by the sheer overwhelming nature of the things he has created by following the blueprints of science and by the organization he himself has established.

People work, they do not live; they do not live, they function. In work they have lost sight of simply how to be. Progress, money and their damnation overcame them. And now, after all his victories, man is beginning to fear himself. Emptiness in man's metaphysical destiny. Escape from metaphysical unease has driven him into a yet more dense jungle and has exposed him to utter desolation.

Man has wearied of the fact that he does not actually exist. He is simply unable to reach himself. Ideological and materialistically hedonistic contamination has caused structural defects in his functions. Man's discovery and realization of himself through self-reliance and in is own strength is a task of Sisyphean proportions. It solves nothing if he transfers from his left to his right hand, or vice versa. The problems of man as man still obtain. A change of place, flag or method alters only the form of the impotence and failure, but heals neither one nor the other. The only resultant differences are in the form of the failures and troubles and in the degree of dehumanization.

After all the steps he has taken through his own volition and strength, man is now his own enemy. His personal, dangerous, breakdown has begun. "Today a man is the ideology for inhumanity" (Adorno). He is a myth which varies from ideology to ideology, a myth which affects only man.

Of all the creatures man is the only one who stands in the way of his own future. An excessive reliance upon reason does not lead to wisdom and life. With the help of reason people are able to organize all manner of things – even their own annihilation. "The heart has its reasons which reason knows nothing of." (*Pensées*, Blaise Pascal). If a man relies purely upon reason he is no more than an intelligent criminal, since reason is invariably the servant of instincts. And so man destroys himself through his own brilliance. By assuming that he is permitted to do anything and everything he is capable of, man has unintentionally set in motion an engine of self-destruction that is moving inexorably towards its terminal destination. Even now it is not certain which poses the greater threat to mankind – misery or progress. One would sooner say that it is progress. The ultimatum of modern science is directed neither at Communism nor at Democracy, but at the whole of mankind. The history of humanity, particularly recent history, shows quite clearly that in moving forward man is not necessarily building himself a road to a better life. Once-famous peoples are now dying before our eyes; once-glittering civilizations are losing their luster while the superior cultures they have created resound. The more a man possesses the smaller he becomes within himself; if he were to have yet more he would become even smaller. If he were to have two mouths he would eat twice the amount and twice as voraciously. Anxieties and worries for his material future are terrorizing man mercilessly. Moral and overall systems of values are in a state of total disintegration.

A diagnosis of the condition of man today runs thus: man has either failed to find himself, or he has lost himself. He is Prometheus, Sisyphus and Faust. The model of man is an alienated human being, a feature which today characterizes everyman. Man's self-realization has failed to come about anywhere. The concrete quality and the universality of suffering, of dissatisfaction, of fear, are all irrefutable evidence that man is a prisoner and has therefore not yet materialized.

Man is constitutionally a dissatisfied creature and also, because of the very heights he has reached, a most wretched and unhappy one. All other creatures are content with their limitations; it is only man who is satisfied with none. Both in his constitution and his desiderata – and especially in his chronic dissatisfaction – he shows himself to be too great to be sufficient unto himself. "Man infinitely surpasses man." (Pascal). He is what he is able to be only if he rises above himself. The complete man is an infinite man. And only such a man is identical to himself. That which remains in him, however great it may be, is merely the beginning, a fraction of him – or perhaps just an image of him. The impotence of man is clearly incurable. Despite everything he has he is a needy creature in search of a fullness of a fullness that in himself alone he can never attain.

To be born means to be thrown into existence. Consequently, man's beginnings are in the hands of another and his purport and aim are determined through the will of the Creator. The realization of his completeness can be achieved only through that same Creator.

From the hands of God man can go but into the hands of God. And everything that he is able to do with himself he may either accept or reject, but always with the greatest of consequences to himself alone.

Man is in the process of creation. Present day man is only a rhizome for the man who is to come, according to the will and majesty of his Creator. This is not a question of the divinization of man, quite the contrary; it is a question of his humanization. A man is not what he makes of himself, rather what he desires or what can become of him. The only quality of any value within him is that which strives for the impossible but against which his efforts, that are purely human in nature, stumble.

Even man's constitutive restlessness and discontent with all he has realized and achieved indicates that he has been created for something greater and higher. By nature he is a Utopian. His one constant thought is that tomorrow he will have, tomorrow he will live. But never today. This shows with absolute clarity that man is not what he is but what he is yet to become. That is his historically-religious dimension. "In man lies the future of man." (Fr. Pauget). Only the insane are happy in this world, since man is not yet a complete man. He has yet to become so. And only when he succeeds in surpassing himself will he become complete. Utopia is not only Utopia but a landmark, and at the same time the most powerful *spiritus movens* in history. When man possesses everything the earth can offer, he will want the Earth. For he is larger than himself. "Man invests immeasurably more than himself into each of his passions." (Fr. Mauriac). "Man is a natural yearning after the unnatural." (W. Kaspar), and therefore "a creature of the future." (ibid.)

The disharmony between man's wants and his actions is, however, quite apparent. Man's self-realization has not only been unsuccessful, it has been impossible. If man is made in the image of God then he belongs more to God than to himself. For as long as man is upon the earth he can be but in a state of promise. The more he belongs to God the nearer to the realization he is. Man is, therefore, enchained only by his own will, for God has offered Himself to man. And man cannot afford to pass Him by because in doing so he is denying his own self. In searching for a god within himself and outside of God, his actual yearnings are a confirmation that he has been searching along the wrong path. Man cannot shed the shackles linking him to God. In fact the more empty of himself he is the better are his chances of being filled with God – for God gives Himself to the hungering. Man's tragedy lies in his desire to be a god himself, and he is unable to fend off the evil that he attracts to himself thereby. Outside God, man is nothing, least of all a fulfilled man.

Humanity orbits around itself instead of turning towards God. The West is beset by atomized individualism, the East by depersonalizing totalitarianism. This is the state in which Our Lady finds us today. And she is hastening to bring help for her lost and confused children.

When children are suffering, to be a mother is still more painful, and this is why Our Lady in Medjugorje is so often seen in tears. But equally often she is full of joy and laughter. This tragedy in which her children are participants and their pathological predilection for the limited and the deadly cause sorrow to Our Mother, while the deep-rooted trust in conversion leading to a legitimate future in Christ causes her joy. She came to help us to find, and to live in, peace. Today, it is not ideologies, doctrines, the clash of interests between classes that need to be reconciled. It is a matter of people's reconciliation with God. Everything else will come solely from that. The final chance of avoiding self-destruction for this generation lies in the acceptance of His help Man is transcendent and this is why he must not stop at the bounds of the world and consciousness. He is a contemporary of the future. That is why he must pass through the present, as a traveller looking for the best road. In a concrete situation on the road to the future Our Lady has offered herself as a stalwart, unwavering companion and a powerful mainstay.

Unfree man

In current times, when the topic most often heard discussed is freedom, there is progressively less of it to be seen. People – even fighters for freedom – are stealing it from themselves. Despite the promulgation and acceptance of the Declaration on Human Rights by the United Nations Organization, the question of freedom continues to represent the most serious single problem in all parts of the world. It is true that some progress has been made, but the actual roots of non-freedom have yet to be touched.

There is a great difference between freedom and freedom. When the word is used people are generally talking of privileges. Freedom to them means that they can do exactly as they wish, and those who do so actually consider themselves to be free. Marx has said that the free man is he who can "hunt in the morning, fish in the afternoon and criticize to his heart's content after his meal." Such a concept implies that every restriction or obligation is a barrier to freedom. The only objective of such a form of freedom is the "ego". Here, the individual is concerned only with himself; he becomes a recluse within himself and centres the universe in himself. He cares simply for himself, his own interests and advantages. And instead of being a free man he becomes his own prisoner. In his nature, however, he is a social animal. His being is incomplete without relationships with others and it is those relationships which set him free. The fundamental relationship is that of love. Consequently, freedom and a love for others are mutually interconnected. Indeed, in accepting love man liberates himself. Love extricates him from within himself and this is the reason why love is a condition of freedom and the path towards it.

To discuss freedom and love is tantamount to discussing God. For we have sprung from the freedom of God. Even before we were able to do a single thing for ourselves the love of God was presented as a gift to us. That same love allows us to grow within it, to mature in fullness. At the same time we invest others with the freedom and love to free themselves. The foundation of freedom is God. A firm and unshakable reliance on Him is faith. With faith man can venture anything and renounce everything in the sure knowledge that his back is always safe. Such a man can truly be free. He no longer has to fear himself or anyone or anything else. He for whom God is everything has no need to feel threatened if he is lacking in non-essentials, or even if they are threatened. Secure in his faith in God he feels no fear of anything else.

Freedom from fear is a sign that a man is truly free. It is things material which have enslaved man. In the practice of life, one maxim has been adopted: What you own is what you are. People think the more they have the more elevated they are. And this is no one-way street – it is also the confinement of and opposition to man's *being*. Instead of a desire *to be,* he is dominated by the desire *to have*. The craving *to have* blossoms into a craving *to have even more*. This craving, known as pleonexia, is an utterly idolatrous service (See Ef 5,5; Col 3,5). It is something more and far worse than simple moral betrayal. Contemporary society is absolutely obsessed with it. The equation reads as follows: more possessions, more bondage; less possessions, more freedom. Since the desire *to have* has become the passion of both rich and poor, a "natural" craving by people for bondage has been created, through their own will and at their own expense.

God, the initiator and creator of human freedom, has been supplanted by possessions. Such a state of affairs must necessarily lead to bondage. Belief in God offers an alternative to the passion for power, possession and sexual self-fulfilment, which leads only to self-destruction.

When man is able to accept God as the ultimate value only then will he be able to freely avail himself of material values. There is no question of despising them or of prohibiting their more prolific distribution – only of our attitude towards them. The problem does not lie in an objective evaluation of material objects, but rather of according them too high a priority in the goals of man. Material possessions and transitory things as such must not represent what they have already come to mean in the conscience of so many people – "you are my sole and entire treasure". This must not be said, either about things or about people. Only God can be man's true and perfect treasure. Man's reliance upon himself and his surrender to selfish instincts for possessions, power and pleasure lead him into slavery and death.

Natural history is a history of death. "Everything must more than merely be." (Sachus). Otherwise, "there is something lacking in everything." (Ingebor Bachmann). Man attains his full dimensions in God. All other restrictions are gyves to man's freedom. And this is why, among the free peoples, there are so few free individuals.

Terrorized man

Terrorism is a malignant but logical phenomeonon that besets man. The disturbed and inverted scale of values establishes different relations. As soon as God and man cease to be ultimate values all else that is constructed in their place causes chaos. And growing chaos will prevail until everything assumes its rightful place. Different orders of values result in changed values, different approaches, different means and different morals. Those who collaborate in the undermining of God's values are collaborators in the degradation of mankind and in the practical imposition on anti-humanistic morals, one of the consequences of which is the terrorization of people.

In no way is terrorism a form of revenge, since its victims are mostly and almost always the innocent. It is in fact a truly loathsome example of anti-humanism which is at the same time pure godlessness – because God is a part of everyman. For the murder of just one innocent person is an assassination of the whole of humanity – and of God Himself. There is something else of far more importance than the man in the consciousness of the terrorist; that is the reason why it is down to pure chance and to the momentary physical incapacity of the execution of the crime that we owe the temporary survival of the human race. As far as principle and selection are concerned, the terrorist's intention is to destroy the whole of humanity with any means at his disposal and without discrimination except, again, by chance.

In the philosophy of terrorism everyone is under sentence of death. And while such a spirit prevails and is active in man, terrorism will not cease – until the last man but one is dead.

Terrorism reproduces itself and obtains its succor through the generation of hatred for others and by the release and detonation of a variety of means and emotions created by it. Thus, moral barriers are demolished and the way is opened to a flood of the most base instincts which, if left to their own devices, would bring the history of humanity to a close in chaos and death.

Today, the fight against terrorism is not only proving to be unsuccessful but also unprincipled and it therefore holds no promise of a favourable outcome. On the contrary, it could be said quite categorically that the anti-terrorists themselves give some degree of support to terrorism, inasmuch as both terrorism and anti-terrorism differ neither axiologically nor as regards their practical execution – as long as God and man are not accepted as the ultimate values and as long as the resultant moral obligation is not binding on everybody. As it is, terrorism and anti-terrorism differ only in the application of means, the number of victims and the tragic quality of the consequences. They are, however, always at the expense of man and in themselves lead to one and the same goal. Actions launched against terrorism, undertaken from the outside, actually promote rather than reduce or thwart it. Since terrorism emanates directly from the heart (See Mt 15/19) it is in the heart that it has to be eradicated and for that external means, particularly those that are terrorist in their nature, are singularly unsuitable. Conversion of the heart requires grace and an acceptance of the love of God and man as the most important and unconditional obligation. This assumes a change in attitudes, axiology and life. The inherent problem here is that people are so totally set in their attitudes and are so utterly trapped by materialistic interests as the supreme norm for everything, that any revision of their positions simply does not occur to them. And even it if does, they remain shackled by impotence and are unable to change anything. This is the basic problem precluding any solution of the situation and which prevents any escape from the vicious circle. The only way out is through conversion.

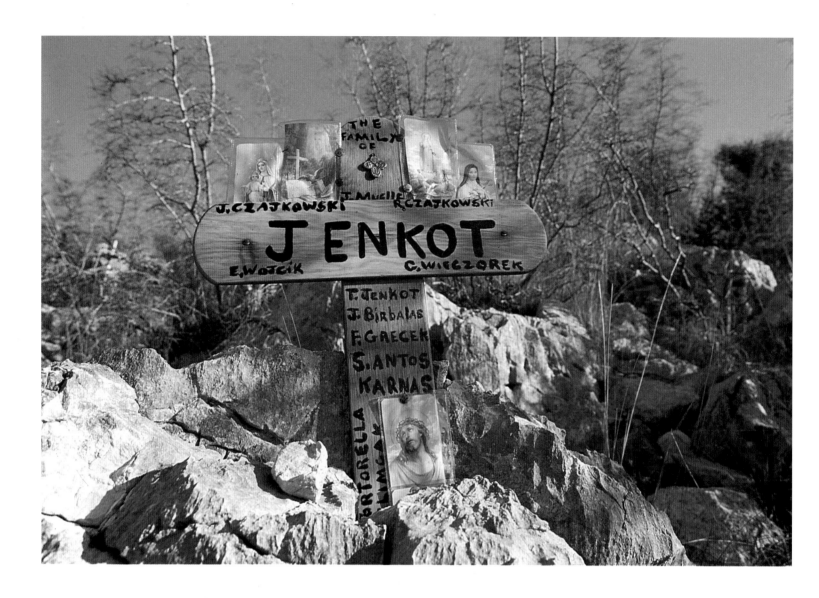

January 25, 1988

Dear children! Today again I am calling you to complete conversion, which is difficult for those who have not chosen God. I am calling you, dear children, to convert fully to God. God can give you everything that you seek from Him. but you seek God only when sicknesses, problems and difficulties come to you and you think that God is far from you and is not listening and does not hear your prayers. No, dear children, that is not the truth! When you are far from God, you cannot receive graces because you do not seek them with a firm faith. Day by day I am praying for you and I want to draw you ever closer to God, but I cannot if you don't want. Therefore, dear children, put your life in God's hands. I bless you all. Thank you for having responded to my call.

June 12, 1986

Dear children! Today I call you to begin to pray the Rosary with a living faith. That way I will be able to help you. You, dear children, wish to obtain graces, but you are not praying. I am not able to help you because you do not want to get started. Dear children, I am calling you to pray the Rosary and that your Rosary be an obligation which you shall fulfill with joy. That way you shall understand the reason I am with you this long. I desire to teach you to pray. Thank you for having responded to my call.

Man mortally poisoned

Today, narcotics are a hellish reality. Mankind does not know enough about them and they are not taken seriously enough. Material interest, devoid of all moral control, has found a partner in human weakness, a collaborator in the ruthless accumulation of wealth with – and serving to exacerbate the problem – the co-operation of the victims themselves to their own detriment. Drugs are poisoning and destroying millions of people, threatening – through an eruption of passions – not only the health of contemporary generations but also the very survival of all normal people.

Addiction to drugs is no longer restricted to specific parts of the world. It has become a common practise among all peoples, from cigarette smoking and the consumption of alcohol – as the most naive forms of dependance – to addiciton to drugs of the most lethal kinds. Of late, interest in those more dangerous drugs has soared and as a result the danger to the whole of the human race, a danger of far-reaching proportions, has increased dramatically.

Drugs are no longer transported by caravans. These have been replaced by caravans of aircraft as, for instance, on the American-Mexican border where one plane can carry hundreds of kilograms of cocaine. In 1977 Carlos Ledher joined forces with Jorge Luis Ocha and Pablo Escobar Gavir, who together formed the notorious Medelin cartel for the production of and trade in drugs, a business competing in its wealth with the largest of American companies and equalling that of General Electric; annual profits exceed three billion dollars.

The skills and might of the drug merchants taxes even the resources of the USA, which itself has poured billions of dollars into the fight against drugs and has seen the loss of the lives of several hundred of its operatives in the process. This massive investment has resulted in a mere 1% reduction in the traffic. Since 1976 the USA has spent 21.5 billion dollars in combating traffickers in drugs. Seventy-six per cent of that huge budget has been spent on the destruction of coca and marijuana fields with herbicides, in the sinking of the ships which sail along the Florida coast and on controlling the border with Mexico. But results are negligible. Amalgamated cartels, linked through the growing and transportation of drugs, have at their disposal electronic equipment designed to counter any monitoring of their activities by law enforcement agencies. Their financial strength is such that they are able to "buy" all witnesses, to corrupt all officers and to have murdered any and all judges. They no longer count their money, they weigh it.

The Mayor of New York, Mr Koch, has stated that the drug trade has reached the proportions of a threat to the nation.

In the United Stated alone, twenty-three million occasional users and one and a half million habitual users spend more on their drugs than the entire worth of General Motors. The drugs they use include cocaine, heroin, marijuana, hashish and hallucinogenic drugs such as LSD, stimulants and analgesics such as PCP (phencyclidine hydrochloride). When the whole world is taken into consideration, a total of millions upon millions of people are dying every year, or are poisoned – some more or less destroyed physically and spiritually. The plague is spreading ever wider; the numbers of victims are increasing dramatically, the fight against drugs is becoming progressively less effective, the trade evermore successful and the general threat to humanity evermore terrifying.

Drugs have become a secret weapon. They are being used to poison and render incapable those countries whose systems and peoples are alien and whose own resources are used to further the process. The drug trade is often controlled by the State, as is the case in Burma, Thailand and Laos. In certain situations the cartels producing and trading in drugs are wealthier and stronger than the States in which they operate, as in Colombia for example. Hashish, which is obtained from Iran, Irak and Afghanistan, is used by various Islamic revolutionary movements for the destruction of all who oppose their ideologies. Hundreds of thousands of people have been drawn into the production of drugs. There are around forty to fifty thousand peasants in Latin America who are working for the Medelin cartel referred to earlier. This cartel possesses a strong and sizeable maritime fleet and the loss of one of their ships to the police has little or no effect on the trade. They also have a fleet of aircraft which makes about 18,000 flights a year over the United States, their pilots receiving at least $20,000 per flight.

The USA has demanded of Colombia on a number of occasions that the drug trade organized by Carlos Ledher be stopped, but to no avail. The barons have responded to attack with murder and corruption. Escobar, mentioned above, has a powerful army equipped with the latest weapons and he has even organized two schools which train assassins. Their victims to date include many anti-drug fighters, among whom are the Colombian Minister of Justice, Rodrigo Lara Bonilla, as well as fifty judges, more than ten journalists and over 400 soldiers and policemen. Legal sysstems are in a state of total paralysis. Police and administrators at all levels have been corrupted. The previous Colombian President said in May 1988, "Last year we were on the edge of an abyss – now we are at the bottom of it." The cartel has organized a network for the laundering of money – whereby the illegal profits are turned into "legimate" banking operations. The center of all these operations has become Panama under the control of Manuel Noriega. He has simply sold the country to illegal drug trafficking and receives millions of dollars in return, from which he apportions massive sums for Cuba and Nicaragua. Many banks have been established whose shareholders include the Abu Dhabi and Bin Mahfouz families from Saudi Arabia.

At the bottom end of this foul and evil trade are children between the ages of ten and twelve who live in the poorer areas of large cities. Attracted by a relatively high income these pauper children become "policemen" for a few hundred dollars, their task being to monitor the movements of the lawfully established police. Their first few dollar thus earned are spent on the purchase of "crack", the latest creation of the drug dealers. The remainder is spent on buying a car. As time goes by their earnings increase and the cars they buy become Mercedes and Cadillacs. If the children are too young to drive themselves, they hire chauffeurs. An extension of all this is the arms trade, which is linked together with criminal activities, robbery, murder and other such "adventures". It is only a matter of time before those children land in jail, demoralized, broken and unfit to go on living. It is from the ranks of children like these, all around the world, that armies of troublemakers are recruited, bringing with them a multitude of problems. Through occasional drug-taking, the users become accomplices in all the forms of crime which could and do occur. The list of those crimes is getting longer and their consequences more catastrophic. Slowly but surely drugs are poisoning the very core of man. They degrade him physically and spiritually and are preparing the ground for the final apocalyptic evils.

Man deprived of his "humanhood"

With his ever-increasing obsession with self man has made himself the supreme standard for everything that surrounds him. The result is a disordered society and the consequences pose a deadly danger to the very survival of man on this earth. Having adopted the principle of pleasure man has forsaken fidelity and the giving of himself in love and sacrifice, and through this he has made impossible both a normal society and his life within it, thereby endangering its very foundations. Love has been replaced by self-adoration, moral obligations by "enjoyment". Marriage and family, the fundamental units of society and the wellspring of people, have lost their bedrock. Real matrimony is becoming increasingly rare; indeed, marriages are ever more fragile and temporary. Instead of there being a togetherness composed of love and mutual giving, marriage is becoming more and more a union of interest and selfishness of two people. Destroyed within himself man has become incapable of bearing children and of raising them. In some western countries there are already more divorced couples than there are married. Hand in hand with this walks the downfall of peoples.

Particularly catastrophic is the pandemic of contraception and the killing of unborn children. Statistics tell us that there are more than seventy million abortions throughout the world every year – losses far greater than in any war.

The killing of the innocent by their own parents leaves the whole of humanity scarred and in trauma. Utterly destructive and anti-humanistic principles have been introduced into society and through their application every person has been left without protection and the right to life. Whether or not somebody is to continue to go on living will be decided on a whim, on someone's pleasure, on material interests and the selfish motives of some more powerful person, until one comes along who is stronger than the strongest. Moral feelings are being extinguished and human actions and reactions are ruled by base instincts which, in practise, do not fall far behind those of beasts. As a consequuence today's world is filled with the most hideous of crimes against man.

In a certain way abortion also kills those who undertake it. It inflicts deep wounds upon their conscience; it seeps into their character – an indestructible maggot to torment the soul; it destroys humanistic feeling and shatters personal harmony; it renders us incapable of giving ourselves to others. How is it possible for people to be loved by those who sentence to death the human being closest and dearest to them – their child. With their psychic and moral structure disturbed they cease to be normal. They are left with no peace, no love and no confidence. Ceaselessly echoing through them is the voice of the murdered innocent and they are unable to exorcize it. Abortion bears witness to be the fact that every such humanism is in actual fact cynicism and moral Pharisaism.

The falling birth rate, a rate already too low, heralds enormous changes that one does not normally consider. Among these changes is the ageing of a people which will have incalculable consequences in relation to the psyche, to survival – the survival both of the people and of the civilization they have created. This danger is particularly grave due to the fact that today's civilization is formed mainly of those who are ageing rapidly because of the low birth rate.

Natura vacuum abhorret – Nature abhors a vacuum. Just who will and how will we fill the current gaps in culture, technology and the population? Tremendous changes are on the horizon somewhat similar to those which occured in AD 5-6 caused by Avar penetration and by the onslaught of the barbaric peoples of the East into Europe. Disparity may result in massive upheavals, which in themselves would solve nothing but would serve merely to break down and level all peoples into a state of deprivation, poverty, misery and who will lack the capacity to direct themselves towards something better.

With abortion and a lack of love, true culture and progress have been undermined. There is not a single idea which could be common to all, or at least to the larger peoples. It is only through the existence of such an idea that it will be possible to unite all categories and classes. It is only in this way that unity could be preserved, notwithstanding material, cultural and civilizational differences. It is not possible to make all people wealthy in material riches; it is possible – although by no means easy – to make them own to the same concepts and the same spiritual values. Otherwise, there is "little use of the egalitarianism of the earth's resources among those who are equal in relation to spiritual wealth." (Leon the Great). All the world is in need of a Saviour – the large and the small, rich and poor. Oblivion, in particular the conscious rejection of spiritual values, will bring equality only in destruction and regardless of all other differences. People "can have the same intention without possessing the same wealth." (Leon the Great). Humanity, which through a low birth rate and the practise of abortion has put a knife to its own throat, is being confronted by the Mother who has come to snatch that knife away.

And when we observe all the troubles and horror of a humanity deprived of its "humanhood", it becomes transparently clear that Our Lady has arrived at exactly the right moment – if not at the last moment. ∎

Tomaž Lauko

Dr Slavko Barbarić, OFM

»...YOU ARE THE VEHICLES TRANSMITTING THE GIFTS«

OUR LADY'S MESSAGES AND TIDINGS

■ Fra Leonard Oreč

The first encounter by the seers with Our Lady occurred on 24 June 1981 on the feast day of the last of the Old Testament prophets, John the Baptist, who baptized Jesus Christ in the river Jordan and who from then on pointed Jesus out as "the Lamb of God who takes away the sin of the world" (Agnus Dei). That first encounter was one of total silence; there was no spoken discourse between her and the seers. She was merely there; and yet without using words she was so eloquent. Her figure, surrounded by a halo of light, stirred the souls of the youthful seers with a sense of joy mingled with fear and uncertainty. Through her uncovering and recovering of the Child she held in her arms in that first Apparition she imparted the most profound of messages in utter quiet: I am with you. I am your mother. I shall protect you.

This kind of feeling was experienced by all the prophets in their initial contacts with divine and supernatural reality: joy tinged with fear, security and uncertainty; the need to meet again and yet a feeling of unease at the thought that the event could be repeated.

The message was a powerful one: she is with us as a mother who protects, defends, soothes and cares.

The second day that she appeared she first signalled with her hand – come closer. This was an invitation not only to the seers but also to anyone who is distant from God to come closer to Him. He is near and, through Mary, calls for a meeting. The seers understood, and with them others who happened to be there. Heeding the call, they ran; they felt no hardness of stone at Pobrdo, no sharpness of thorn upon which they stumbled. When God calls, all paths are smoothed. And everything we walk upon is transformed into a path that leads to Him. It is enough for man to respond, to move; as it was sufficient to set so much in motion in the young seers and through them, initially, the parish and subsequently in so many throughout the world.

Many wonder why Our Lady appears every day – although not every time with a message. It is this very renewal of a daily presence, seen but unheard, that makes it all the more precious. It teaches us, each and every one of us, to support the other; in silence and simplicity, together with the next person who lives and wants to live in the fullness of his life. Thus a mother even though she may be saying nothing does indeed speak, and in volumes. Her mere presence imbues us with a feeling of security and cultivates a place for peace in our hearts.

On the third day they saw her standing by the cross in tears, and this time they did hear her voice – "Peace! Make peace! Peace!"

Her tears were an eloquent portrayal of the condition in which humanity finds itself today. Every tear is pregnant with symbolism, a metaphor of motherhood. As once she stood by her Son's cross on Calvary and now on the Mount of the Apparition, she implies that the world itself is crucified; that she loves it with all the tenderness of a mother, that she is heroically faithful. In standing by the cross and pointing to it she is guiding the whole world onto the most secure path towards peace. Only in the presence of the cross upon which one dies, with love and that is borne by love and that symbolizes a willingness to make sacrifices for others, are we able to hear the true words of peace; and it is only there that the words may be understood in their true and full import. No other pulpit such as this exists. In other words if a preacher of peace is not prepared to die forgiving, he will undoubtedly preach measure for measure; encouraging conflict, instigating war and directing destruction.

To her tears and the cross, Mary adds an invitation to peace. In turning his face from God man has opened the gates to the deepest unease. In searching for a form of peace that does not accord with the peace of God man has imperilled himself, his people, humanity and his entire environment. This is why, when Mary calls for peace, she is calling for a reconciliation with God. For only in God, in the source of total reality, will man be able to put to rest the anxieties which are leading him astray and to destruction. And in turning to God, discovering peace, he will also begin to discover enjoyment in his peace with his fellow man and with nature. This peace is like a river that springs from divine love, flowing through the heart of every man; gently laving away all layers of fear and leaving the heart pure and able to live in quiescence. A new internal strength awakens, fortifying the man; drawing him back from desolation, eradicating embitterment and preparing him to accept a new reality.

A drug addict who has managed to rid himself of the habit described his experience so: "Up until the moment I felt this profound sense of peace in my heart and a joy that I had never known before, I would prepare for myself a daily cocktail of hell – heroin, alcohol and tablets. But now, there is not a thing that I would exchange for this feeling of peace."

And it is in the name of this peace that Mary the Queen of Peace calls to us. It is not just that we should avoid war; we must avoid all forms of destruction and begin afresh with a new strength. With this new peace we shall create new relationships between people within the new accord with God and the whole of nature. In this God-given peace emmities will become new friendships, distrust will turn to comradeship while pride and selfishness will become transformed into service in love and simplicity. The family becomes a community of happy individuals who love each other, and humanity a community of brothers and sisters. Mary's daily motherly presence, her tears and pleas for peace, have already moved multitudes, setting them upon the path of peace. But the final goal is still far away – and the road is hard. And this is why she has declared: "I am tireless!"

Convert

"Convert and believe in the Gospel." It was with these words that Jesus began His public work and ministrations. And in the same way so Our Lady began in Medjugorje. She has called to peace and has shown the way to that peace – through conversion. By repeating the call and by indicating the way she has become one with the order of prophets.

The call for conversion indicates in a special manner that God is love and mercy itself. The basis of conversion is not the human need for such, but rather the love of God which forgives and which through forgiveness wants to save. The road to peace exists and can be negotiated – God is confirming this fact through Mary, the Queen of Peace. Conversion is possible because God is not able to abandon us – we who are His beloved creatures whom He has created and to whom He is eternally committed – to the fruitlessness of a failed existence.

The call to conversion given by Our Lady at Medjugorje is telling us the following:

– to hear God's voice in Mary and through it to turn to God, who not only waits for us but who is ceaselessly searching for us;

– to hear the voice of one's inner being and to perceive that without the God who loves us our life will remain hollow, and that by following the deepest of our yearnings we are actually searching for God in everything;

– to experience and to admit the fact that our sin of straying from God and that of our disobedience to His will destroys and ruins us, and we must summon the whole strength of body and soul to find a way out from the wastelands of one's own living, and to embark upon the new road towards peace;

– to live a life of love, justice, peace and mercy, creating the necessary equilibrium between spiritual and material values – that very equilibrium which is disturbed by sin;

– to find a place in one's heart both for God and for people and to accept them, gladly, as brothers and sisters, as children of one Father in one great family;

– to expand in our usefulness to other people, particularly the ailing, the poor, the deprived, the persecuted, the confined, the unfree;

– to have the strength to love not only our friends but also our enemies, and to forgive those who have offended us;

– to do everything with love and in joyous hope to expect the fulfillment of the salvation and redemption that God offers us in Jesus Christ, and in this joyous hope to build a new and better world.

■ Fra Jozo Zovko

Conversion is, therefore, the growth of man to the limits of God's intentions, and an initiation in being able to open himself to God's influence.

It is, then, the matter of a man who is "all of a piece", who could become ever more patterned on God Himself but who has been enmeshed in evil. In the process of conversion the evil is suppressed and the convert is purified of its consequences. Along this road, one must:

– overcome arrogance of heart and be rid of all arrogant behaviour and not seek personal advancement at the expense of others;

– prevail against implacable irreconcilability with God and with other people and in humble coexistence surmount every conceivable conflict;

– eradicate the urge for destruction and begin building a new world by healing the wounds of the soul resulting from destruction;

– resist the temptation of abusing power and might, of wealth and knowledge and invest the totality of one's strength in the service of others in the light of God's love;

– shun the tendency to choose the easy and less unpleasant options in personal, family and social life and to apply those solutions which demand a positive and personal involvement;

– resist the temptation to misuse the gifts of technology, medicine and other sciences; avoid all manipulation of people and stand before God in true humility, since man is neither a maker of norms nor a lawgiver to the world; on the contrary, the world has merely been entrusted to him for its safekeeping.

Jelena Vasilj is one of those who, without Apparition, have been receiving messages with their heart and she describes her experience in this way:

"Until recently I thought that haughtiness was the desire to be seen, to strive to be the centre of attention and the like. But that is not haughtiness; to be truly haughty is to deny God the first place in one's life."

To become a convert, therefore, means to become a real person, to perceive and to accept one's true place with regard to God and towards other people. For man to embark upon this road and to experience genuine conversion he must be involved in a change in order to evolve as God conceived him. And in this man is in need of God's help, the gift of God's life, the grace of God. This is the road to which Our Lady calls us, a road on which man will rise above himself, becoming more and more – and yet more – a man closer to God, in order that he may live in a love whose fruit will be peace.

■ Fra Jozo Zovko

Pray, pray, pray

Throughout the messages of Medjugorje and the discourses of Our Lady at the time of the Apparitions the word most frequently used is "prayer". A question is in order here – one could ask why it is that Our Lady speaks so often of prayer, when she herself has said that her primary and main goal is peace? The answer lies in a true understanding of prayer. A prayer is at one and the same time an encounter and a conversation with God – and God is the source of peace. This meeting with God through prayer is like the meeting between a flower, the sun and water; a union of the thirsty and the wellspring; of the hungry with a banquet; of the lonely with a friend; of a child with its mother. The meeting with God through the medium of prayer can be compared to an embrace from parents we have not seen for a long time. Ultimately it comes down to this – are we, to whom Our Lady speaks, really going to meet God in prayer?

Of course it is possible for one to pray but to fail to meet God, just as it is possible for a thirsty man not to find the spring for which he seeks. The cause of this failure is not that the spring is concealed; the fault is to be found in the manner of the search and in the choice of path. In other words a believer can remain a captive, torn apart, terrorized even and fettered by a life devoid of meaning and joy, to be forever unconverted and without peace. This happens when prayer is superficial, irregular and listless, with no real yearning for God. Prayer is, therefore, firstly a search for God and only later does it result in a meeting with Him. The search itself moves and disturbs us; happiness producing a restlessness within us. It is not satisfied either with half measures or with wrongly directed efforts. It is for such encounters with genuine and deeply-felt prayer that Our Lady in Medjugorje calls through her messages, and educates us through her continuing presence.

■ Marijana Vasilj

Decision

In this school of prayer in which Our Lady is the Mentor, the curriculum begins by making the decision to embark upon the search for God and to take the road that leads to Him; and this is a two-way journey – for He is also moving towards man. When, through the first Apparitions, the invitation was made to repeat "the Creed, and the Lord's Prayer seven times", many were surprised and asked why, and wondered what it could mean. It is known that through those prayers Our Lady is confirming the ancient practise of invoking commendations (locally known as preporuka – family prayers in which the souls of the departed are commended to God) within Catholic Herzegovian families. The emphasis on repeating the Creed is of immense significance in a period where masses of those who are experiencing a reawakening of the need to believe know very little – and that only superficially – of what the Church really believes. This wide-spread ignorance in some

areas concerning the content of the Creed goes hand in hand with erroneous information regarding faith, an ignorance which stems from confused thinking in some areas of the Church. It is equally important to realize that the Creed, in addition to explaining basic religious truths, embodies the decision of accepting the faith not only as a revelation of God, but also an acceptance of God and the entrusting of oneself to Him. The Latin verb *credere* (to believe) is derived from the word *cordare* – to give one's heart – which means the complete giving of oneself and of being at another's total disposal. It is a question not only of theoretical but also practical tuition in spirituality. To repeat the Creed each day in prayer is a daily practise in the giving of oneself to God, to be fully aware every day of the meaning and the orientation of one's entire life. The repeating of the Lord's Prayer seven times contains a concealed call to perfection, to the fullness of prayer and spiritual life, since in the symbolism of the Bible this number implies fullness.

Say your rosary

As the Apparitions began to increase in frequency, the call to prayer uttered by Our Lady asked for more than just the Creed and the seven times repeated Lord's Prayer; the plea came for us to say our complete rosary, every day and all its three decades: the joyful – Hail Mary; the sorrowful – the Lord's Prayer, and the glorious – Gloria Patri. It is obvious that prayer must permeate our every living moment and that we are unable to fulfil this duty merely through recitation of this or that number of prayers. It would not do to think that the call to say the whole of the rosary is a fixed rule on how much one should pray in order to have done enough. The call is, in fact, a guidance to merge the path of our life with that of Jesus, a command that implies that everything we undertake must become part of our life lived in God's presence. To observe Jesus and Mary through the course of the fifteen Mysteries of the rosary is to be one with them along our road through life, to learn from them all that we still do not know, to be always ready to give and to sacrifice, to seek ceaselessly for cause for joy in our life and ever to celebrate the Resurrection.

Pray with your heart

Early on in her talks with the seers in Medjugorje Our Lady called on them to pray with their hearts. The young, who from the beginning have understood that Our Lady has recommended them to do what their forbears did in their family prayers, must not be a mere repetitive recitation of devotional utterances. A believer must not liken himself to an eastern prayer wheel, into which a written prayer is placed and which is then left to the wind to turn, each revolution of the wheel representing a repetition of the prayer. The call to pray with one's heart means that every prayer has to be a personal experiencre, a statement of personal ideas and thinking, a true union of thought and life with God.

To be able pray with one's heart is a very special grace that God grants to those who begin seeking Him daily, who devote time to prayer and who accord it its rightful place.

■ Vicka Ivanković

God comes first

Our Lady's call for unceasing and heart-felt prayer does not mean that we must all become brothers of some strict monastic order – who do indeed spend night and day in prayer and prostration – but we do have to adopt new attitudes to life, to learn a new approach towards people, towards God and towards creation. Those who learn to truly pray with their hearts will become equipped for new relationships with their fellow men, relationships growing out of love and which are characterized by compassion and justice. Such people will be able to resist the tendency to become arrogant and will avoid creating within themselves their life's programmes according to self-seeking motives, and will instead seek for and find in prayer the will of God, their whole life programme, which they will be able to fulfil from day to day, from one opportunity to the next. Their first inspiration will be God; in other words they will discover meaning in their life through God and will live according the same laws He lives by. The Gospel tells us that God is Love. Surely, therefore, such a man will not live solely for the purpose of acquiring wealth and fame nor solely for pleasure, but rather to offer and give of himself to others – to God and to his fellow man – and in his own receiving will continually regard whatever comes his way as a gift; to give happiness in his giving and to be grateful for the given. Such an attitude to life – which is, in fact, a true god-like semblance – can come only from a heart which gives itself utterly to God. Once man begins to live God's way, then his whole life and everything about him will begin to change in the image of God. And *this* is wherein the advent of a new and better world lies.

Fast

In Medjugorje Our Lady has also asked us to fast. She has pointed to the irreplaceable value of fasting. With this appeal she is in fact echoing the prophetic call of John the Baptist and of all the prophets. She has reminded us of the words and the practise of her Son, Jesus. The Medjugorje call to fast is expressed in the directive that a believer should adhere to a truly rigorous programme of fasting twice each week on bread and water. In these times of ours, blessed as we are with modern medical achievements, it is unnecessary to try to convince people of the great benefits to physical health that are to be gained from such fasting. On the part of the believer fasting is primarily the realization of his own power of self-control, a practical proof that he is not enslaved by the passions and demands of the flesh but rather that he is able to subdue them. In this world, threatened as it is with so many approaching ecological disasters, where the very food we eat is becoming increasingly contaminated – in part by pollution, in part by unnatural processing and storage – the importance of fasting on bread and water has become almost imposed upon us. This is the most natural of foods to be found within the whole of our cultural environment – bread. And this is the drink which symbolizes purity, simplicity, naturalness –

water. It is a symbolic call directed at all of us – to be natural, to be pure, to live life, and not just to act it.

The fast is, therefore, also an invitation which prompts us to treat with proper respect all created things, particularly food and drink, to be able and to know how to enjoy them for what they are in the knowledge that they are only the fuel of life and not the point of life; that they restore life's forces and bodily reserves and are not a form of addiction. It is a matter of living out our life in this world in a sober and dignified manner and using all the gifts that God has given us, but without being enslaved by anything. In all religions the practise of fasting is an indispensable part of the spiritual aspect of life. Discipline with regard to food and drink permits the reawakening of capabilities in man which have become dormant. He who fasts obtains sharper perception, a greater overall command of his senses and, in some cases, the ability to triumph over illness both in himself and in others. Cleansed by fasting we are also able to discover the secret of the Eucharist – not only with our heart but also with the innermost core of our being – as well as being aware of the presence of Christ in the sacrifice and feast of the Mass symbolized by bread and wine. And in this awareness of the secret of His love we grow; we become more able to meet with our fellow men and to live with them.

■ Fra Filip Pavić

The days to be set aside for fasting are, according to the traditions of the Church and to the recommendations of Mary, each Wednesday and Friday. Friday, because it was on a Friday that Christ died on the cross and is why this day has always been commemorated in the Church by fasting and by other pious acts which express a joint suffering, as well as our readiness to suffer with Him. These are statements of our solidarity with God who has, out of solidarity with us, accepted suffering. Wednesday is, as dictated by the rhythm of the days of the week, better suited to be a day of fasting. But it is also interesting to note that, according to ancient tradition, it was on a Wednesday that Judas attended a meeting with those opposed to Jesus, and there betrayed Him. Thus, our fasting on that day constitutes the final expression of our faithful unity with the betrayed Saviour and with all who have fallen victim to treasonable acts.

Faith

When Our Lady in Medjugorje calls to faith, when she stresses the need for belief, then her call is – as we have previously pointed out when speaking of the Creed – far more than a mere invitation to become familiar with chapter and verse of our faith, more even than having an exact knowledge of what the Church believes in and what it commands should be believed. Her call to faith actually involves and includes every one of her pleas that we should allow ourselves to be led by God, to surrender ourselves to Him, to open our hearts and to allow God's word and love to change our whole being. Faith is not just cognition and an intellectual standpoint, it is actually a form of friendship – a trusting and reliable friendship with God.

The call to belief is a plea to all the faithful to resolve the contrasts between their faith and their lives, not to believe in word only but to search endlessly to the last spark of one's strength – with a faith of such strength as the force with which God makes Himself known to us through deeds. And in this strength find the understanding for new and improved, more just and more merciful solutions, solutions that would be in the true spirit of Christ.

Marianic spirituality

In addition to the main messages, which we can understand as elements of the same overall mosaic, in her messages given on one Thursday in each month Our Lady has of late begun to fit into the picture further pieces, by means of which she is illuminating and clarifying her road to peace. These are words and messages, calls and warnings, encouragements and reprimands, that are understandable if we accept that Our Lady is teaching her children gradually to understand and follow her spirituality, teaching them to live the way she once lived.

While we recognize in the messages of peace, conversion, fasting and faith, an invitation from Our Lady to walk with her, the Mother, the Queen of Peace, in many other of her words we are also able to discern an educator and instructor, one who thinks of everything and who tirelessly endeavours to correct and mend our ways.

In such messages Mary often calls on us:

– to be grateful that she is yet a further expression of our faith and service to God. Mary often thanks her seers. Gratitude is truth in humble simplicity but lacking in any self-humiliation. It is from Mary's prayer "My soul gives praise to the Lord" that we are best able to see what that humble gratitude was; how it clearly saw, recognized and accepted God's gifts with all the joy of life. The gratitude which can accept God and the people about one in such a manner is an unavoidable condition for peace;

– to a saintliness which should suffuse every second of her children's lives, a saintliness which is deeply rooted in spiritual and physical well-being, in the healing of our inner selves from the consequences of sin. This saintliness includes an unqualified readiness to love God and our fellows without reserve; to be prepared to forgive unconditionally and to be the first to make the move; to look for God in everything and above everything;

– to read the Holy Scriptures and to celebrate Holy Mass. Mary wishes our meeting with Christ in words He had spoken and in the Eucharistic symbolic presence through bread and wine to be a genuine exchange of gifts with God, who presents the whole of Himself to us in the very death and Resurrection of Christ in order to receive us as an offering. The call to a Eucharistic encounter with Christ is fundamental and radical. Mary wants our life to become a Mass for others, just as in the same way Christ became in His moment of sacrifice;

– to combat Satan since it was she, Mary, who at the beginning of the Bible was indicated as being the Woman who would, together with her offspring, crush the head of the snake, symbolized as the source of sin and death. Satan, the unseen evil spirit, is at work today also. Make no mistake, he is powerful; he is a generator of trouble and a sower of the seeds of dissent; he provokes hatred, is an instigator of wars; he fights against and persecutes salvation. In Medjugorje Mary speaks clearly of this danger, this foe. For as long as he is working her role must remain forever active. For as long as the evil one pursues his attacks on her children her fight to protect us against him must continue. In her messages she very often admonishes and calls, comforts and encourages her children to be tireless in the battle against Satan. From many of her messages it is quite clear that Mary calls upon us to align ourselves with God in the war against Satan, promising ultimate victory to every one of her children. And the victory she promises is that of peace.

And in the end peace will mean victory over every evil and sin, when – as the Holy Scriptures promise us – all will be subject to Jesus, who will present it to the Father. Death and every enmity will be overcome and the Kingdom of God will arrive. Mary the Queen of Peace calls to us daily and she is doing all she is able in order that it will be so. And she enlightens us so that we may be able to understand that each one of us, every single individual, is an indispensable factor in that final and inevitable outcome. ■

Tomislav Rastić
Jelenko Rastić

Dr Slavko Barbarić, OFM

BELLS OF A THOUSAND TEARS

MEDJUGORJE ECHOES THROUGHOUT THE WORLD

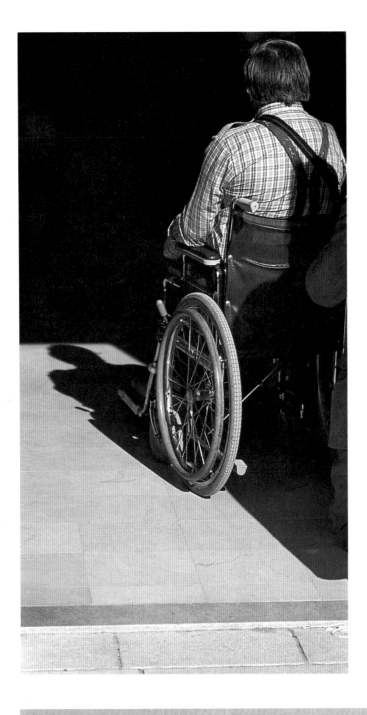

"If events in Medjugorje are to be taken as facts then one of the most apparent acceptances of this would be the river of pilgrims that, against all manner of trials and tribulations, began to flow as early as the third day – but especially from the fourth day – of the Apparitions of Our Lady. On that day several thousand pilgrims, or onlookers at least, gathered here. Since that time the river has flowed unceasingly, albeit from time to time alternately ebbing and flowing, but with each passing day becoming evermore colourful.

I believe that there is not a single continent on earth able to "boast" that it has resisted the attraction of this mysterious call. No one will be able to really explain this procession of more than a million, comprising people from all walks of life – from the maimed and the poor to the most exalted of experts – but all will have to admit that the Eternal Director has surely staged it all with exquisite and impeccable inspiration, as only He knows how..."

Those are the prophetic words written by Fra Janko Bubalo in his book *A thousand encounters with Our Lady in Medjugorje* (Jelsa, 1985). The river of pilgrims has widened year by year and they come from everywhere. In would be impossible to estimate the reverberations and effects of the movement inspired by the Medjugorje Apparitions and oriented towards Medjugorje. The fact remains that this spiritual movement has spread throughout the world faster than any other within the Church, and that it is producing multiple results – continually, powerfully and in increasing strength. To observe and judge the phenomenon of the Medjugorje Apparitions in isolation from the context of the massive spiritual movement it has generated would be completely unobjective and unscientific – worse, it could only produce an untrue picture.

The Prayer Groups

The first to feel the strong impact of Our Lady's call to prayer was the community of the parish of Medjugorje. Now, many believers from the parish come every day to evening Mass. It has become their regular daily gathering in prayer, through which they are experiencing continuing and systematic spiritual growth. In addition to these gatherings, however, several other prayer groups are active. The first such group was formed on the first anniversary of the Apparitions when, as the seers Ivan Dragičević and Marija Pavlović have testified, Our Lady asked them to form a group and to pray for her endeavours, for the realization of her goal. This group is still active today, meeting for prayers usually in the hills either on the Mount of Apparitions, or on Križevac. Another prayer group meets three times each week in the premises of the parish office and has been active since the spring of 1983. This group was formed by Jelena Vasilj, a young girl with the gift of inner voices, in which she experiences in her heart messages from Our Lady, although Jelena does not see her. The group gathers around Jelena every day.

These calls to form prayer groups have been heeded not only in Medjugorje; their echo has resounded around the world. Although we have no reliable information as to the number of prayer groups that have been inspired by Medjugorje, it can safely be said that they may be numbered in their thousands, founded by pilgrims who travelled to Medjugorje and who felt the call to prayer. According to the information that we do possess, some of those groups attract more than two thousand believers each week. Their programme of prayers is, for the most part, patterned on the evening prayers held in the Medjugorje Church: long prayer prior to Holy Mass, participation in the Mass followed by the saying of prayers for healings. Some people also prostrate themselves before the Holy Sacrament or in front of the cross. In Austria alone there are more than five hundred Medjugorje prayer groups and in Italy over a thousand. There is any number of groups in all the countries of Europe and on other continents.

"Oasis of Peace"

Following his experiences in Medjugorje, Professor Gianni Sgreva, a priest belonging to the Monastic Order of Passionists, began to assemble a specific prayer group from which spiritual professions are born. On 7 June 1987 – this was the beginning of the Marianic Year – having sought and obtained the blessing of his superiors and that of the Holy See, he gathered around himself about twenty boys and girls. Their programme is inspired solely by the messages from Medjugorje. They began their activities in Priabona, Vicenza. This group today has over forty members and is working in Toscana. Some of the group are already studying theology. This community, known as the "Oasis of Peace", intends to take in many more members as soon as their premises will allow. The group is contemplative and action–oriented and its membership is becoming increasingly multinational.

Centres for Peace

The pilgrims who returned home from Medjugorje began to spontaneously spread the Medjugorje message of peace. Thus inspired, centers for peace began to spring up in various countries and today they number more than three hundred. In Vienna one such center is called The Prayer Action of the Queen of Peace. A separate community of volunteers involves itself in publishing activities; yet another is organizing pilgrimages and a third is developing as a prayer group.

There is an active center in the distant land of The Philippines, known as the "Centre for Peace – Asia", which began its activities in 1988 and which is composed of laymen and priests, most of whom have been to Medjugorje; their stated desire is to promote peace throughout The Philippines and the world. They began to call the people to prayer and fasting and presented themselves to the local population through a night-long vigil in the cathedral in Manila that was spent in prayer, and with a procession through a section of the city. The procession and the vigil was repeated on the seventh anniversary of the first Apparition in Medjugorje.

In the premises they have been given and which have been blessed by Cardinal Sin of The Philippines they hold a daily Eucharist. On the second and fourth Thursday of the month they conduct three-hour prayer sessions (which they call "intensive prayer") during which all three decades of the rosary are said; Mass is celebrated and the congregation prostrates itself before the Most Holy Altar Sacrament, special prayers being said for healings. On the 25th of each month they organize huge gatherings to pray for peace and for peacemaking. Every Monday special prayers are said for all those who devote themselves to the propagation of peace. Participants have the opportunity of attending the confessional and of receiving spiritual guidance each Monday, Wednesday and Friday.

The address of the center for peace in The Philippines:
Centre of Peace – Asia
3rd Floor, Facilities Center
Shaw Boulevard, corner Old Wack Road
Mandaluyoung, Metro Manila

We have gone into some detail in describing the center in The Philippines, but all such Medjugorje centers for peace, in whichever part of the world they may be located and where they are active, have their own individual history and their own similar programmes.

Publishing activities

All around the world, Medjugorje, its Apparitions and its messages have been responsible for the publication of a host of books, booklets, studies, magazines and newspapers. And already it is possible to find, in the office of the parish priest of Medjugorje, books that have been published in more than twenty languages. They also have papers there printed in more than thirty languages. The editions of a number of books have reached into the millions and some of them are in their twentieth reprint.

The testimony of journalist Wayn Weibl – a Lutheran who made the decision in Medjugorje to enter the Roman Catholic community – appeared in the summer of 1988 in the form of a small booklet. More than seven million copies have been sold to date and it is still in great demand. There exist monthly publications with a distribution of more than 200.000, among which is *L'eco di Medjugorje*. The magazine *Queen of Peace* comes out three times a year and its sales total 600.000 copies. The Society of Friends of Medjugorje in Milan has published four books of deliberations which are, in fact, Italian translations of the Medjugorje sermons given by Fra Tomislav Vlašić and Fra Slavko Barbarić. This Society has found sufficient funds to allow for the free distribution of the books. Translations of the same books have been published in German, French, English, Spanish and Portuguese. One small booklet, entitled *Pray with your heart* has, in less than twelve months, been translated from the original Croatian into the following languages: Italian, German, French, Dutch, Czech, Polish, Hungarian, Spanish, Portuguese, Basque, Japanese, Korean, Tibetan and Tagalo (one of the languages of The Philippines).

July 25, 1987

Dear children! I beseech you to take up the way of holiness beginning today. I love you and, therefore, I want you to be holy. I do not want Satan to block you on that way. Dear children, pray and accept all that God is offering you on a way which is bitter. But at the same time, God willreveal every sweetness to whomever begins to go on that way, and he will gladly answer every call of God. Do not attribute importance to petty things. Long for heaven. Thank you for having responded to my call.

February 25, 1988

*D*ear children! Today again I am calling you to prayer and complete surrender to God. You know that I love you and am coming here out of love, so I could show you the path of peace and salvation for your souls. I want you to obey me and not permit Satan to seduce you. Dear children, Satan is very strong and, therefore, I ask you to dedicate your prayers to me so that those who are under his influence may be saved. Give witness by your life, sacrifice your lives for the salvation of the world. I am with you and I am grateful to you, but in heaven you shall receive the Father's reward which He has promised you. Therefore, little children, do not be afraid. If you pray, Satan cannot injure you even a little, because you are God's children and He is watching over you. Pray, and let the rosary always be in your hands as a sign to Satan that you belong me. Thank you for having responded to my call.

On film and on television

The news of the Apparitions in Medjugorje is also broadcast around the world through the media of film and television. Many visitors have made any number of video-cassette recordings which have been copied in many parts of the world. Crews from the best-known film and TV companies have also made a considerable number of professional documentary films here. The USA's most popular TV programe *Twenty-twenty*, which has an audience of around twenty-five million, has sent its experts to Medjugorje on two occasions to record material for their show. BBC London made a lengthy documentary film which it broadcast on the highly-rated programme *Everyone* and which was hugely successful, arousing great interest among viewers in Britain.

Over radio and telephone

Don Mario Galbiati of Arcelasco, near Milan, began sending news and messages with a small radio transmitter, naming his station *Radio Maria* which he operates with the assistance of several volunteer helpers. Over the few years following the inception of his undertaking and working exclusively with volunteer help it developed into a large and powerful organization tirelessly disseminating the message of Medjugorje, calls to prayer, reflection and effective love. The messages are transmitted directly from the office of the parish priest to hundreds of thousands of listeners.

A special feature, or a concurrent phenomenon of the events in Medjugorje, are the telephones that are specifically used to spread the news about the Apparitions and messages from Our Lady. These telephones are located mostly in private houses and the Centres for Peace mentioned earlier. The process usually begins when an individual or an enraptured family places a private telephone at anyone's disposal, and during a given period of the day anyone may use their telephone to listen to a recording of the latest message from Medjugorje. When interest rises and those who are willing make it possible, new contracts are signed with the local postal authorities, or with telephone exchanges, to arrange for the same line to have several extensions so that a number of people may call in at any one time. The Prayer Action of the Queen of Peace in Vienna, referred to previously, has made arrangements for four hundred people to listen to the Medjugorje telephone simultaneously, while from the city itself the number can be dialled free of charge. This was made possible by the management of the exchange when it was realized just how many people were phoning that same number.

"MEBA-MEB"

Worthy of special mention are the activities of "MEBA" (**Me**djugorje per i **b**ambini **a**bandonati – Medjugorje for abandoned children). This action was started by the Italian priest, Giuseppe Sometti, following an experience he had in Medjugorje – a very powerful thrust to lead a much more intensive and priestly life. He claims that messages from Medjugorje have inspired him to begin caring for abandoned children in this way.

The Swiss pianist, Mauro Paris Harsch, testifies that he has experienced both conversion and healing in Medjugorje. In one of his letters he writes: "When I returned from Medjugorje I saw for the first time in my life that the poor exist." His first act was to form MEB (**Me**djugorje per i **b**ambini). The artist now donates all the proceeds from his concerts to this charitable institution. Within the honorary community of the institution are many famous figures from public life, such as Franco Zeffirelli, Sophia Loren, and others.

Travel Agencies
in the service of the pilgrims

It is no surprise that the millions of pilgrims attracted the attention of a great number of travel agencies in many countries. Special air routes were organized and established and countless buses, ships and ferries became involved. It can be said that every travel agency of any standing, both at home and around the world, has involved itself in this massive movement. JAT (Yugoslav Airlines) announced in 1989 that it is to produce a special film for the anniversary of the first Apparition, which will be screened for passengers during longer flights.

The Medjugorje Apparitions and their messages have certainly sent powerful echoes around the world, and their effect is primarily conversive and peace-making. They result in bringing to the surface the essential goodness in mankind, they change those who have not listened before into people of goodwill. It can really be said that many have already turned their swords into ploughshares, and there have been many swords drawn against the Apparitions of Medjugorje. However, the power of the message of peace has helped many to understand that this was indeed God's work, that peace is possible and that it depends on the efforts of every individual. A message which resounds so forcefully, so widely and so deeply must surely have an extremely powerful source. It is difficult to imagine that a natural phenomenon alone – if we were to try to explain the Medjugorje Apparitions and messages as some mysterious but natural and deeply-hidden aspect of an individual or collective psyche – could generate such supernatural, humane and compassionate effects. Here, there is no question of establishing group, regional or national selfishness; of the elevating of one above or before another. It is a question only of the Evangelical messages of peace, justice, the love of truth and of ubiquitous brotherhood. And this is why the echoes of Medjugorje are being heard by communities of adherents of other religious faiths and by those with different outlooks on life. This message mellows differences, breaks down prejudices, brings closer together peoples of all persuasions and of the most diverse of religions and cultural backgrounds. In itself and apart from all else, this is a sign that God is at work. ■

Tomislav Rastić
Jelenko Rastić

Dr René Laurentin
Živko Kustić

CROSSES OF LOVE

A TESTIMONY OF SCIENCE AND THEOLOGY

Dr René Laurentin, a French priest, noted theologian, publicist and reporter, Professor at the Catholic Institute in Paris and at Dayton University in the United States of America, is the best-known European and world authority on research into Apparitions of Our Lady. He has spent several decades studying all such Apparitions – from those in Lourdes to the most recent elsewhere. It is no great wonder, therefore, that he turned his attention to events in Medjugorje. He has written and published a number of books on the subject, either on his own or in co-operation with other scientists – in particular from the field of medicine. We have asked Dr Laurentin to provide for this book a short summary of his experiences and to give his thoughts on the matter. The interview with Dr Laurentin took place on 27 February 1989 and was conducted by the Chief Editor of Glas Koncila, Živko Kustić.

Why does Medjugorje attract the attention of scientists?

Q *During the past few years you have devoted yourself to a serious and in-depth study of the phenomenon of the Apparitions at Medjugorje. Just what was it that led you to decide, on the basis of initial reports to reach you, that this event deserved your scientific attention bearing in mind that similar claims are made in other parts of the world?*

A It did not take long for me to realize that the Medjugorje Apparitions were something quite new: Apparitions in the East, irresistible Apparitions... and – at the outset at least – support from the Bishop. On 23 February 1982 I wrote a short article for *le Figaro* in which I gave a brief informational summary. In 1983 I had the opportunity of questioning a number of Croats at the International Mariological Congress in Malta. I found them to be very circumspect. It was from them that I learned about Father Rupčić, a recognized expert in interpretation of the Bible and who had written a book about the Medjugorje phenomenon. I requested that the book be translated for my library on Apparitions (OEIL Edition).

The *le Figaro* article created problems from the French public, which demanded less circumspection from me. This demand became more vociferous following publication of the Croatian book and I had to face it. I wrote to the Bishop who, back in 1981, I knew was sympathetic to the Apparitions. After visiting him I was confronted with the realization that his views were now completely different. I took his reservations seriously and from there I began my own evaluation . My ultimate findings were positive but out of respect for the Bishop's position and in deference to scientific prudence I forbore. This is the reason for the interrogative nature of the title of the Laurentin-Rupčić: *La Vierge apparaît-elle à Medjugorje?* (Does Our Lady Appear in Medjugorje?). The book became a best-seller with more than 100.000 copies sold in France, Italy and the USA. There were two things in the beginning that particulary impressed me: the results (the quality of prayer, the high number of conversions, the spiritual enthusiasm, etc.), and the limpidity of the seers (their obvious mental health, their frankness in both their day to day life and in their ecstasy).

I am especially sensitive to the latter since the pseudo-scientific studies of Doctor Charcot – who induced ecstasies (exclusion of the outside world) in hysterics in his psychiatric practice – have spread the belief that ecstasy is a pathological phenomenon. Photographs of some occurrences of apparitions (not recognized) – twisted necks, contorted and cataleptic postures – appear to confirm that diagnosis. Certain theologians have concluded: God can manifest Himself in the pathological also. This conclusion which today is favored by many has always seemed to me to be amphibolous, erroneous even, and for the following reason: if God visits man He certainly does not do so in order to make him sick, but rather to heal. Experience confirms that where God visits a pathological individual the condition is improved. I have confirmed this in Medjugorje itself, where several mentally retarded pilgrims had experiences of profound grace which they related to their escorts more lucidly and intelligently than one could ever have expected from their normal mental state.

First-ever medical examinations of believers in ecstasy

Q *How does the scientific study of the Medjugorje Apparitions and seers carried out until now differ from studies to date of other such phenomena?*

A Bearing in mind the Bishop's unremitting opposition, my positive evaluation demanded all the more verification, since I was intent upon respecting his point of view. No medical research into the state of ectasy had ever previously been undertaken. I therefore requested doctors to carry out just such a research. A possibility existed for co-operation with Henri Joyeux who, in 1984, was only 38 years old. In 1985 he was the recipient of the Antoine Lacassagne International Award for Cancerology and in 1987 he became the youngest member of the French Academy of Surgery. I asked him if he would carry out tests never before performed on normal seers in ecstasy: encephalograms (which make possible the pictorial recording of all activity in the eight key regions of the brain), electro-oculograms, etc. It was a kind of medical "premiere". Italian doctors have since repeated those tests and confirmed the original findings, enriching the research with a whole battery of new tests. These tests have confirmed that when in a state of ecstasy the seers are not asleep, they do not dream, they are not in any kind of pathological state. It constituted a true scientific and theological revolution in research into ecstasy. Hallucinations were also excluded. All this I told to the Bishop of Mostar in the summer of 1984 and I was very surprised that he had not taken in into consideration when he gave his much-publicized statement of October 1984. Later on, however, in January 1985, he wrote me a frank letter in which he said: "It is not hallucinations that I wish to stress. That was the interpretation of one of my doctors. I now believe that it was something worse – simulation."

But our tests also ruled out the possibility of simulation. The conclusions were wholly confirmed at an international assembly of French and Italian members, including the President of ARPA, Sig. Luigi Farini. Twelve reports on medical findings plus ten theological reports signed by myself were sent to the Pope and their receipt has been acknowledged. This information has been conveyed to Cardinal Ratzinger and is one of the reasons why the negative opinion of the local Bishop was not accepted.

Doubts dispelled

Q *What was it about all that happened in Medjugorje that most arou-sed your scientific and theological suspicions? What was it that disturbed you most about the behavior of the seers and their surroundings? Where you able to allay those feelings, and if so, how?*

A It would take us a long time if we were to discuss every one of the many serious suspicions and objections I had, but they have been resol-ved and now belong to the past. Step by step I investigated all the doubts that arose, specifically in the eight volumes of *Dernièrs nouvelles* (Latest news). Most of the seers are above criticism, and even if I had seen two of them to be waverers it was quite understandable in persons so young and living under conditions that were really insufferable. When we consider the truly impossible conditions in which they do live (disturbed constantly by the Commission, by doctors, by the pilgrims),

it would not be surprising if the seers *were* to be mentally unstable. I have never relaxed my recommendation that they should be allowed at least Saturday off to be left in total peace, just one day each week; it is my fervent hope that this has been implemented by now. It is known how Ivan – rather timid and very frightened by two members of the Commission – extricated himself rather clumsily from a session of que-stioning that was too much for his spiritual strength to support by using a naive and fabricated excuse. He bitterly repented his weakness ... it was in fact a far lesser weakness than that of St Peter (s. R. Laurentin, *Dernièrs nouvelles de Medjugorje* No.4, 1985, pp 17-23).

Q *Of all the results of the scientific research, which of them have most confirmed your conviction that the Apparitions were real?*

A My diagnosis is primarily a spiritual one, in accordance with Evangelical and Christian traditons of discernment. Scientific tests have made valuable contributions, particularly in confirming that there is nothing of a pathological nature to be found in the seers. But in themselves they do not make it possible to categorically state: this is Our Lady. The researches that were carried out threw a deep and penetrating light onto the recipients. In my book *Medical and Scientific Studies of the Visions in Medjugorje* which was written together with Professor Joyeux (the only one of my books to be translated into Croatian!) I have demonstrated that many indicators of the objective apparition agree with the fact that our sense organs continue to transmit stimulations from the outside world; stimulation which, it might be said, do not reach the cortex, that is to say, they do not penetrate the seer's consciousness. I will not go into a detailed explanation here about the hypothesis of this type of cognition, which is objective, although different from the regular one. Not only is the Apparition no less real to the seers, it is even more real than the normal world. Their return to this world is for them not a form of awakening but rather a return to a passing reality to which they are, as it were, quite well adapted.

Private revelations with a public impact

Q *Are you not troubled by the fact that Our Lady of Medjugorje appears too frequently – every day, in every place that any of the seers happen to be?*

A This is a serious objection. During the Plenary Session of Bishops held three years ago in Lourdes, one of the Bishops said to me: "Five years of daily Apparitions – that is proof enough that it is not true." He did not hear my answer out. It is true, though, that throughout the entire history of the Church (in which Apparitions have manifested themselves with different characteristics and which have been mostly discrete and private affairs) many seers experienced Apparitions or messages throughout their whole lives. Visions are quite involuntary. One cannot regard the Apparitions of earlier periods on the basis of the contemporary model of Apparitions, which have a quite different meaning, not only mystically but also prophetically, containing messages for the Church and the world. These new characteristics in themselves change the meaning of theological speech which presents those Apparitions as private. Contemporary Apparitions have acquired a public meaning. In order that this duality of expression be rectified, I would suggest we call them special revelations, to differentiate them from the Revelation of Christ. They are nothing more than references to the Revelation, in different times and in different areas of the Church.

News after Fatima

Q *In your opinion what are the specific qualities of the Medjugorje Apparitions which differentiate between them and others known and recognized?*

A I would say that Medjugorje is one stage of that path. Following the messages on prayer and conversion (the Miraculous Medal, la Salette, Lourdes) Fatima added a prophetic orientation for the conversion of a world going through very difficult times. In the opinion of Mgr Franić, Medjugorje is a continuation and a reinterpretation of Fatima, which is sometimes distorted in the cause of the anti-Communist political crusade. Medjugorje is a call for a solution to the difficult problems of agnostic atheism in the West and of ideological atheism in the East in a royal manner – through love. The Blessed Virgin also brings a new principle of ecumenism of love which extends further than ecumenism of dialogue. Along just those lines Mgr Franić has received a strange message (for which it is difficult to establish a critical basis): "Love your brothers the Serbs and the Orthodox; love your brothers the Muslims; love those who rule you." This enduring, peace-making love has proved itself in deed. It has become a testimony and it has been understood. The Yugoslav Government could conclude that Medjugorje is a purely religious phenomenon, not political, and is therefore legal. This is an outcome of no negligible proportions as far as the future reconciliation of East and West is concerned.

Seers are not infallible

Q *Are there any discrepancies in the accounts of the seers and if there are how could they be explained without the whole phenomenon being compromised?*

A There have been, as there always is in multiple testimonies, approximations, interpretations, frictions, intimidations or misapprehensions – any or all of which could be seen as contradiction. I have already mentioned the case of Ivan. This may be where Vicka received the Blessed Virgin's words supporting her ardent defense of the two Franciscans disciplined by the Bishop. The question applies equally to the ten secrets and to the great sign which, according to the seers, is to appear on the mountain, and also to Mirjana's statement that those Apparitions will be the "last", while subsequently Apparitions which seem to be real began elsewhere (as described in my book *Multiplication des Apparitions.* Fayard, 1988). There is nothing here that gives rise to any confusion in my mind. Prophecy, even the true one, is often arbitrary, approximative, exaggerated. It takes short cuts and exceeds its aims. All this is the very essence of prophecies; they make revelations but they are not infallible. I have my reservations about the details referred to earlier; the future will reveal whether they will be proved true or otherwise. It would be premature of me to pass judgment now, if only because of insufficient knowledge regarding the secrets. The message requests us to be fully cognizant of how serious the situation is in which the world finds itself and which in diverse ways is destroying itself. In my books I have made mention of this message many times and it would serve no purpose to repeat it here, but I would like to draw attention to my study entitled *Message et pédagogie de Notre Dame à Medjugorje.* Differentiation between the message and pedagogy is an important criterion in evaluation.

As far as the second part of your question is concerned, it is difficult to evaluate how much of it all is interpretation and projection on the part of the seers. It is obvious that they are reliable in all the essentials, but they are not infallible.

Q *What are you able to say about the messages of Our Lady in Medjugorje in relation to the specific and contemporary reality of the Church around the globe and in this part of the world? Does it not sometimes happen that the seers relate, in the name of Our Lady, that which they think she would say?*

A Again, it is difficult to say how much of it is their interpretation and their projection. They articulate freely and simply under pressure of an avalanche of questions that is both wide-ranging and aggressive. I would like to reiterate that they are clearly credible in essentials but they can err in detail and it is equally clear, therefore, that they do not share Papal infallibility. The fundamental messages from the first six days – about God, conversion, prayer, fasting, peace and reconciliation – can all be considered as absolutely irrefutable. They have been verified both in the life of the people and of the Church.

Miraculous healings

Q *Has there been any working of miracles in Medjugorje, or in connection with it, which meets the normal criteria of the Church?*

A I would say that until now there have been two cases of recovery which satisfy conditions asked for in Lourdes:

Firstly, the recovery of Diana Basile (atherosclerosis) matches the criteria of more than three such recoveries recognized in Lourdes and about which I have talked at great length with Professor Thiébault, a renowned specialist in the disease. The Basile case history is much more current and comprehensive and comprises 150 documents. In Milan twenty years ago it was possible to conduct many more tests than was previously the case – far more advanced than those shown to me by Professor Spaziante – and under optimum conditions (Diana Basile was a hospital employee).

Secondly, Dr Korljan believes the recovery of Damir Čorić to be even more convincing (because it was more apparently organic). Tomograms have established that in his case a reconstruction of degenerated brain tissue has taken place. Dr Antonacci, who was sent to Medjugorje to set up a Medical Bureau there, estimates that among the 350 cases of recovery that have been registered with the office of the parish priest (the case of Diana Basile, publicized in Italy, is not included among them) there are about twenty which are different in their content, are of considerable importance and which can be considered as complete. It is a matter for personal regret that Dr Mangiapan, President of the Medical Bureau in Lourdes, voices through his responses in interviews a negative judgment regarding those recoveries and with which he is only partially familiar. It would be no bad thing if he were to come to the site, to come with an open spirit, with a truly scientific approach and without any fear that Medjugorje in any way poses competition for Lourdes. Lourdes is developing admirably and will continue to do so. Having remained devoted to Lourdes, to which I have given more than twenty years of my life, I answered the Bishop of Lourdes, Mgr Théas, when questioned on the subject: "For me, it is the same." Just as Catherine Laboure, a seer from du Bac street, said when she learned of the Lourdes visions. Let us put away parochial conflicts, this rivalry between various sanctuaries – from which I myself have suffered. May the Almighty grant that all misunderstandings, springing from all kinds of passion, evaporate.

Is it Mary resurrected?

Q *In your opinion is what the children are seeing Mary resurrected in her true form, or is it something else?*

A The six seers in Medjugorje see Our Lady as a real person (as did Bernadette). They were able to touch her. For them it is no dream, which is also confirmed by encephalogram. She is no less real, indeed she is far more real, than the everyday world.

Jelena clearly distinguishes her own visions (with her "heart" – which means that they are intimate, internal communications) from the objective visions that the seers experience outside themselves, which are three-dimensional, tangible and incontestable.

I am aware that in speaking like this I will appear naive and that I shall be attacked for it. Such a reaction is inevitable until the philosophical hypnotheses related to the subject have been revised (as I have endeavored to do). We are all, some more than others, susceptible to the idealism which became prevalent after Kant and Hegel. This philosophy aims to reduce everything to the subjective. It is agnostic to the "thing-in-itself". This inability to face what is real (particularly in the matter of religion and the Incarnation) is a serious malady in our culture and our Church. Both our civilization and our faith need to return to realistic philosophy, a philosophy that will not be naive but which will evaluate the authenticity and the relativity of human knowledge regarding ordinary reality and the reality that God manifests in mysterious ways, through Apparitions of Christ or the resurrected Virgin.

What does the future hold for Medjugorje?

Q *What could be the destiny of the Church in Medjugorje?*

A It is too early to judge the future, particularly before the Church authorities announce their decision. My hope is that the judgment of the Commision will not be impaired by fear or by convention, either in relation to people or to circumstances. It seems that it would be rather difficult now to make a negative judgment with any honesty. That would be to contradict God's grace which ceaselessly gives of itself in Medjugorje – through the seers to the parish and to the pilgrims. I believe it probable that the cult established in Medjugorje will be recognized, a cult which does exist, which is peace-loving and in which so many Bishops have taken part. Prudence and diffidence will no doubt result in an extensive period of waiting for the Apparitions themselves to be recognized.

Whatever the case may be, we must beware the triumphalist illusion which could engulf one's soul, faced with such abundant new grace of the Holy Spirit. We could be tempted to think that this is to be a new period of history, substantially different from the past – after the fashion of Joachim de Flore – or an utterly new and wonderful future. Whatever there may be in the secrets that is miraculous, God does not act as a magician, but in humility, as in the Gospel: from the Incorporation, through public life to the Passion. It remains to be seen, therefore, where God is taking Medjugorje. What matters is that those Apparitions have released massive waves of prayer and conversions (of tens and hundreds of thousands) and recoveries (of hundreds) and on a larger scale yet seen this century. Medjugorje has moved the younger element of the Church in unprecedented numbers – hundreds of thousands of Christians have travelled to Medjugorje from as far away as the USA and The Philippines, passing through West Germany, France, Italy, etc. May God sustain this enthusiasm, that it does not diminish as happens in other places. Medjugorje is, like all other great spiritual movements, linked to human weakness and it will become worthier in humility rather than in triumphalism. I myself have suffered for Medjugorje – calumnies, a State process culminating in punishment ... I do not blame anyone, although my reputation has been damaged. I am prepared to endure more suffering (as are many others) for the wonderful work of God that is unfolding in Medjugorje. The priests of the parish have my greatest admiration since they – each with his own specific charisma – know how, in extremely difficult circumstances, to avoid the catastrophies which dog their every step. They have succeeded because for them it is God, the Blessed Virgin and prayer that matter. They have also borne the consequences courageously and unswervingly; how, I really do not know. I know of apparitions which have been wasted due to deviations. I have already said how worried I was about Medjugorje back in 1984-5. Manifold trials and tribulations imposed by both State and Church have transcended human strength and I admire the skill of those priests that has guided them through Scylla and Charybdis. ■

Archbishop Dr Frane Franić

INSPIRATION FOR
CONTINUING CONVERSION

I first went to Medjugorje on 21 December 1981, there being several reasons leading to my decision that I should go.

Two Jesuits, Father Tomaso Beck of Milan and Father Faricy, an American Professor of Spiritual Theology at the Gregoriana Papal University in the USA – visited me *en route* to Medjugorje and suggested that I should go there myself. I felt it prudent to heed the advice of two such esteemed theologians.

Many of the faithful from my Split-Makarska diocese had already begun their pilgrimage to Medjugorje and I felt a responsibility towards them – should I allow it to take place, or should I forbid them?

Then Split became a transit stop-over for many Italian pilgrims along their journey to Medjugorje, among them being many highly-qualified individuals, some of them expert theologians and professors at the Medical Faculty of Milan who began to supply me with documentation regarding their scientific research of the events at Medjugorje. The positive nature of their opinions had to have some influence on me. Personally, as a believer and as a theologian, I have always been interested in such phenomena in the Church. During one particular period I paid three visits to Father Pio in San Giovanni Rottondo. I have studied the works of the Jewish-French philosopher Henri Bergson who had derived proof of the existence of God exclusively from the facts about mystical phenomena among the mystic saints. This is particularly expressed in his book *Deux sources de la morale et de la religion.*

Because of my position at the High School of Theology in Split where I have been teaching New Testament and Dogma, I was also interested in the Medjugorje phenomena from the aspects of both those theological disciplines.

Although I went to Medjugorje exclusively in my capacity of Archbishop of the Diocese of Split-Makarska, I was fully aware that I would be asked about Medjugorje by my colleagues at the Bishops' Conference of Yugoslavia. This was yet another reason, therefore, for my visit – that I might be able to tell them something from my own experience and insight.

As a result of my visit to Medjugorje and inspired by the piety and devotion I directly witnessed there, I came away with a positive opinion. On the evening of the day of my arrival I attended Holy Mass in the Medjugorje Parish Church together with the congregation. The church was full to overflowing – particularly with the young – and the officiating Franciscan priest preached in complete harmony with Catholic doctrine. I must confess that I was pleasantly surprised since I had arrived with preconceived notions expecting possibly to hear some uncertain theological, neological and dubious interpretations of the Bible. The congregation prayed with deep unction and many attended the confessional. Almost all present – and as I said earlier, the church was completely filled – received Communion. All was peaceful and orderly; there were no excesses, the liturgy was in total accord with all the norms of Church practice.

Why, then, should I prohibit pilgrims of my diocese from travelling to Medjugorje; people who wanted to pray there and to go to confession? Particularly when I have seen direct evidence of great and numerous conversions, of prayer and of fasting on bread and water. Many among my own congregation have begun to fast, especially the young, who have started visiting Medjugorje and who have formed a prayer group in Split.

At that time I was not acquainted with the Medjugorje seers or, indeed, with the local Franciscans.

In the following year, in 1982, I continued my visits to Medjugorje with the aim of getting to know and to understand the phenomena better. During the course of my visits i came to know the Franciscan brothers, of whom I previously had had a very critical opinion because of their disobedience of the Decree "Romani pontificibus" issued by Pope Paul VI on the division of the parishes of Herzegovina. To this day I regret that the Franciscans of Herzegovina did not readily obey that Decree, but I lay no blame for that on Medjugorje. I also met the seers – at that time there were six of them. Throughout the course of that year I was present on several occasions during their prayers and states of ecstasy and I can in no way accept the possibility that those children were attempting to deceive. I am convinced that they truly see and hear something that is genuine, that they are not acting and also that is genuine, that they are not acting and also that the Franciscans themselves are not tricksters and are not pursuing material gain.

I also met Abbot Laurentin and have read his books on Medjugorje.

During that same year I remained in contemplation and uncertainty regarding the supernatural quality of the events in Medjugorje. At the beginning of 1983 I personally had a profound experience of prayer, as some sudden and penetrating enlightenment which in a certain way was perceived with the totality of my being, intellectually as well as purely existentially, that God is LOVE, that the Church must therefore also be LOVE, that Mary is LOVE (as of a mother) and that I myself should – particularly as a Bishop – also be LOVE towards God and towards all people: my congregation, priests (diocesan and monastic), towards our Orthodox and Muslim brothers and towards those who do not believe. Then and there I realized that I was not that kind of person and that I should change radically, that I should cleanse myself of all impurities both physical and spiritual, of my prejudices, of my too hastily formed and atavistically embedded opinions – particularly in regard to society as it is and which for us is composed of peoples of different nationalities, religious beliefs and outlooks on life.

This experience was so profound that it is still with me today as a permanent inspiration for continuing conversion, for love, prayer and forgiveness, for penitence as far as my health will permit and for a continual striving to improve my services as a Bishop.

I have always believed that the just and merciful Judge would not cast me into the depths of hell for holding so firm an opinion of the events at Medjugorje. Following my personal experience at Medjugorje I have become convinced that the Holy Spirit is present there and that through His most innocent and most Holy Lady – the Virgin, the Mother Mary, the Queen of Peace, – He gives His grace, faith and love, thereby working for the restoration of the World and the Church.

It pleased me then and it still does today that pilgrimages to Medjugorje not only have not ceased but are actually increasing, even after seven years. I believe that in this phenomenon we are seeing the manifestation of the true religious feelings of believers – *sensus fidei fidelium* – as one of the proofs in favour of Medjugorje. It is therefore with great hope that I am awaiting the judgment of the Holy See, in the trust that it be positive. But however the judgment goes, I shall accept it unconditionally.

I have the opinion that no obstacles exist for approval to be granted for the congregation of believers in that place and that Medjugorje will immediately be granted freedom of the cult – *libertatem cultus!* ■

TESTIMONIES

Personally I am deeply convinced of the apparitions in Medugorje and am deeply grateful... I am deeply convinced that Medugorje is the continuation of Lourdes and Fatima... Step by step, the Immaculate Heart of Mary will triumph. And I am also deeply convinced that Medugorje is a sign for this.

Cardinal Frantizek Tomasek, Archbishop of Prague, Czechoslovakia, Medugorje; Gebetsaktion nr. I, 1988

Medugorje's theology rings true. I am convinced of its truth. And everything about Medugorje is authentic, in a Catholic sense. What's happening there is so evident, so convincing."

Cardinal (designate) Hans Urs von Balthasar in an interview with Fr. Richard Foley of London's Medugorje Center For Peace

I was deeply moved by my pilgrimage to Medugorje.

The late Cardinal Timothy Manning, in a March 3, 1989 letter to Queen of Peace Ministries regretting that he couldn't attend the National Conference aat Notre Dame in May of '89

I am grateful to Our Lady of Medugorje... I know that many people go there and are converted. I thank God for leading us during these times in this way.

Mother Teresa of Calcutta, March, '89 Mir Monthly

In Medugorje we see that the Blessed Mother has agaion renewed the practice of Confession. Now *that* can't come from Satan; otherwise we would have to kiss his hand and say, 'Keep it up!'

Bishop Paul Hnilica, S.J., Auxiliary Bishop of Rome. Medugorje: Gebetsaktion nr. 3, 1988

The fruits are so obvious, so clear and impressive, both within Medugorje as well as with those who have returned home from a visit there, that they simply cannot be ignored.

Most Rev. Seamus Hegarty, Bishop of Raphoe, Ireland, Medugorje: Gebetsaktion, nr. 1, 1988

I love Medugorje!
Most Rev. Myles McKeon, Australian Bishop, Medugorje: Gebetsaktion nr. 2, 1988

We three bishops and 33 priests will travel tomorrow from Medugorjeto Rome... Coming from Brazil we had only one desire: to come to Medugorje and spend a week in Mary's school... we never dreamed that so many and such beautiful graces were awaiting us!

Bishop Murilo Kieger, Santan Caterina, Brazil in a homily on January 21, 1988 in St. James Church in Medugorje

Here (in Medugorje) I had experiences which greatly impressed me; I want to remain in Mary's school."
Comments made by Bishop Angelico Melotto at the conclusion of a November, 1988 retreat with Archbishop Franic, Bishop Chinole of Malawi (Central Africa) and 136 priests in Medugorje. Queen of Peace Journal, March 1989

I am convinced that Mary is appearing at Medugorje.
Bishop Michael D. Pfeifer, O.M.I., Diocesan newspaper of San Angelo, Texas, April, 1989

I'll be glad to speak on 'A Bishop's Perspective on Apparitions', but nothing is going to keep me from giving my own personal testimony that Mary is really appearing in Medugorje!

Bishop Nicholas D'Antonio in response to the request that he speak at the National Conference on Medugorje at the University of Notre Dame in May, 1989

In the private discussions I had with the Holy Father... (he) spoke very favorably about the happenings at Medugorje, pointing out the good which it has done for people.

August 5, 1988, Diocesan Pastoral Statement on Medugorje by Bishop Michael D. Pfeifer, San Angelo, Texas

'Holy Father, I have just come from Međugorje. There are wonderful things going on there...', and the Holy Father told me, 'Yes, it is good for people to go to Međugorje and pray and do penance. It is good', he said.

Bishop Sylvester Treinen during Sunday's homily at National Conference on Međugorje, May 14, 1989

Without question they (the apparitions of the Blessed Mothewr in Međugorje) are fully genuine.

Msg. John Magree, secretary to Pope John Paul II, Medugorje Reflections, Fr. Bob Bedard, Koinonia Enterprises, 1989, p. 85

Never have we seen the church packed with so many daily Masses as now. We are seeing the fruits of what is happening, (i.e. Međugorje).

Archbishop Gregory Young's comments during his June 25, 1988 homily in the Cathedral of Singapore, celebrating the 7th anniversary of the Apparition at Međugorje

Her piety is like a deep, quiet, strong river.

Archbishop Philip Hannan commenting on his Interview with visionary Marija Pavlović, The Mir Response, *July, 1989*

Međugorje has more than proved itself. ... I'm convinced Međugorjewas given us by God. Our Lady was sent by Him to renew the entire Church... Our Lady of Međugorje is giving us the remedies for a complete renewal fo society.

Mother Angelica, May, '89 Međugorje Messenger   ■

■ The parish church – St. James

First National Conference on Međugorje

"Thank you for responding to my call!"

About 7000 Christians who are trying to respond to the Blessed Mother's call gathered last May 13–14 at the University of Notre Dame for the first National Conference on Međugorje. Those present came from 49 of the fifty states, as well as from several foreign countries. When they walked out of the modern basketball arena of Notre Dame's Athletic and Convocation Center, most agreed that they had been touched that weekend by Our Lady and her Son.

For the first time in nine years (and only the second time in recent memory) the "Lourdes Grotto" on the campus was filled with thousands of pilgrims, who had marched in procession from the football stadium and across the university grounds. The normal soft glow of the vigil lights before the statue of the Immaculate Conception spread almost to the lake across the roaad, as some 4,000 of us sang, prayed and received a solemn benediction, each holding his own candle.

The conference began on Saturday morning. Each session began with the recitation of five decades of the rosary. Saturday morning we also celebrated Holy Mass. Fr. Edward O'Connor, C.S.C., a theologian from Notre Dame and one of the directors of Queen of Peace Ministries, spoke on "Mary's Message to the Modern World". He showed the continuity and development that can be found in the modern-day apparitions, explaining how Mary has appeared on the one hand as the gentle, comforting mother and on the other as the sorrowful and urgent prophet of repentance. After him, the prominent theologian and mariologist from France, Fr. Rene Laurentin, spoke on the Church's evaluation of apparitions.

After the lunch hour and a presentation on the history of the apparitions by Sr. Isabel Bettwy for those who were not familiar with the story, the afternoon session featured talks by Bishop Nicholas D'Antonio on his personal experience with Međugorje and by Fr. Kenneth Roberts on Međugorje and youth. The session ended with a moving multimedia presentation by Tony Cilento, "Portrait of Our Lady". The conference reached its first spiritual peak on Saturday evening, when after testimonies by Wayne Weible and Jan Connell and talks by Denis Nolan and Fr. Philip Pavich, Fr. Pavich led the assembly in the singing of the Chaplet of Divine Mercy and then offered a solemn benediction. During this very worshipful time, many of those who were unable to receive the Sacrament of Reconcillation earlier, due to the huge crowds, went into the arena concourse or one of the gyms to become reconciled with God.

Sunday morning was a time of opening up the vistas as Frs. Harold Cohen, S.J. and George Kosicki, C.S.B., spoke on the context of the Church in which these apparitions are occurring, relating the events of Međugorje to such other phenomena as Eucharistic adoration, charismatic renewal and the papacy of John Paul II. They were followed by a panel in which questions submitted by conference participants were discussed and answered.

The second spiritual peak and the climax of the conference was on Sunday afternoon, as the weekend closed with a liturgy celebrated by Bishop Sylvester Treinan and the crowning of the statue of Our Lady. The devotion that issued forth two days earlier in the drizzling rain in the Grotto and which has ripened and deepened during the next day and a half of talks and prayer came to a deep emotional and spiritual focus right at the end. Bishop Treinan lifted the traditional flowered tiara and placed it on the slightly bowed head of Mary's statue as Bishop D'Antonio lead thousands in consecrating themselves to the Immaculate Heart of Mary. The arena then broke out into a spontaneous "On This Day, O Beautiful Mother"! It would be hard to contemplate and Pentecost Sunday (and Mother's Day) bringing more joy to the Holy Spirit! ∎

"IF I WASN'T A POPE, I'D BE IN MEĐUGORJE ALREADY"

The Auxiliary Bishop of Rome, Mgr. Paul Hnilica, S.J., in the April, 1986 issue of *Madre di Dio*, states that he had gone to Međugorje many times in order to investigate the apparitions. "I wanted to examine and understand what reasons the one who talks against Međugorje and is opposed to it had for doing so. I am convinced that this is a case of slandering... Upon my conscience, I must come to the conclusion that the voice of God is speaking with power at Međugorje."

In the Fall of 1986 the Bishop wrote an article published in *Međugorje: Gebetsaktion* (nr. 4), in which he stated: "The more I have gone to Međugorje and the longer I have spoken with the children, so much more am I personally convinced of the genuineness of the apparitions... When signs like Međugorje happen before our eyes it is the obligation of every Christian to take a stance concerning them."

On April 21, 1989, Bishop Hnilica, who meets privately with the Pope once a week, gave a video taped interview while on pilgrimage in Međugorje. He said that upon recently returning from a meeting in Moscow on behalf of the Pope, John Paul II admonished him for not stopping in Međugorje on his return trip to Rome. The Auxiliary Bishop of Rome reported that the Pope concluded his admonition with, "If I wasn't a pope, I'd be in Međugorje already!" ■

Jakov Bubalo

THE CHURCH IN HERZEGOVINA

The entire area of Herzegovina is subdivided into 17 local districts and 76 Catholic parishes. Of the latter, 15 are located along the left bank of the Neretva and belong to the Diocese of Trebinje – Mrkanj. Sixty-one parishes are situated on the other bank and are within the Diocese of Mostar – Duvno. Both diocese fall under the jurisdiction of a single bishop whose seat is in Mostar. The left bank of the Neretva is known as Eastern Herzegovina and where Croats are in the minority; the population of Western Herzegovina (on the Neretva's right bank) is almost one hundred per cent Croatian. Pastoral services in Eastern Herzegovina (on the Neretva's right bank) is almost one hundred per cent Croatian. Pastoral services in Eastern Herzegovina are performed by the diocesan priests, while in Western Herzegovina they are performed almost exclusively by Franciscans.

Christianity came to Herzegovina in its early centuries, as we know from the many remains of early Christian churches that are scattered throughout the region, referred to earlier. History also records that in the 3rd century, Bishop Venantius died the death of a martyr in the Duvno range. And in the 6th century Duvno was the site of the then active ancient Diocese of Duvno.

With the arrival of Croats in these lands Christianity was to become firmly entrenched. Its roots went so deep that despite all the subsequent persecutions, no matter how prolonged and bloody they were, from Turkish times right up to the present day, the faith of the people never wavered and was never in the remotest danger of being eradicated.

Beginning in the 13th century, the sons of St Francis of Assisi, the Franciscans, began to take it upon themselves to be the pastoral guides of the people in Bosnia and in Herzegovina. From that time onwards they started to develop and to expand their pastoral and all-encompassing cultural activities through the lands of Bosnia and Herzegovina, winning the hearts and minds of the local populations by their dedication, self-denial and by their closeness to the people. In addition to carrying out their religious duties the Franciscans were also known for their role in educating the people, as doctors and as all round guardians of the wretched local populations. In the 14th and 15th centuries they built a significant number of churches and monasteries throughout Herzegovina. It has been historically confirmed that in those times Franciscan monasteries existed in Mostar, Konjic, Novo (near Čapljina), Ljubuško and in Blažuj, near Duvno.

In the days prior to the Turkish occupation a special sect known as the Bogomils was active and widespread throughout the territory of Bosnia and Herzegovina. In the view of some historians it was here that a special Church of »Bosnian Christians« was born and flourished. Was it really an heretical sect, or was it merely composed of neglected and deserted Catholic faithfuls? The science of history has not managed to fully answer that question to this day. One might say, however, that they were just ignorant and unenlightened believers rather than notorious and destructive heretics. The fact remains that in those distant and confused times the bearers of true faith, Dominicans and Franciscans, were also active in the region of Herzog-Bosnia in restraining the latent Christian heresies and in spreading the true Catholic teachings.

When the Turks conquered Bosnia in 1463 (and Herzegovina 13 years later), however, they were to bring with them a centuries'-long period of hardships and anxieties for the Christian populations of the two regions. It proved to be an era full of suffering and of martyrdom but which was at the same time equally full of wonderful examples of how to live and to die for the glory of the Cross and for precious freedom. And people were dying all over these mountainous and rocky lands from the very earliest days of Turkish rule. By as early as the 16th century Turkish flames had totally consumed all the Herzegovian churches and monasteries and Turkish blades had struck down many a Franciscan Father. There followed an almost three centuries-long indescribably hard and fateful period during which not a single church or any other roofed place of worship could be found anywhere in Herzegovina. In that twilight of man's love toward his fellow man and humanity it was especially difficult to provide spiritual sustenance to uphold the faith among the tormented and weary people. Not only were there no churches in Herzegovina, but there were also no places of congregation permitted for the people where Christian services could be performed. In times of such unparalleled troubles the Franciscan friars persisted, which demanded more than mere human courage and sacrifice. In the dark and silent nights they travelled secretly and in stealth to join their forlorn and deprived flocks to offer spiritual uplifting and to encourage. They came on foot from their distant retreats, wending their secretive way through gale-swept gorges, braving the dangers posed by wild beasts and stealing into sheltered, concealed and previously organized places of worship beneath the skies. Onces there they would celebrate,

together with the faithful, the Eucharistic Service of God and from that place they would travel onwards carrying inspiration and the word of God to those too weary to meet them in the mountains. In the course of such nomadic spiritual ministrations the Franciscans would find succour and temporary abode in the poor family huts of their grateful followers. And should those Franciscan priests – disguised in local folk costumes – happen to be stopped and questioned by Turkish gendarmes, members of the household would present them as Uncles, thereby saving them from inevitable Turkish punishment. It is from that ancient practice that the special name »the Uncles« came, to describe Bosnian-Herzegovian Franciscans and which until this day survives as a term of endearment among the simple Christian folk of these parts.

Generally speaking, the centuries of Turkish tyranny was a period of darkness and pain for the Christians of Bosnia and Herzegovina. The Herzegovina of those times was as some rockbound Golgotha, whose ascent was eternal. It trudged endlessly through its interminable night of impenetrable darkness, waitings and yearning for that first light of dawn. And the additional burdens it carried were the waterless rocks and the droughts which spread starvation. All its tortured days, its unhealed wounds, all the miseries of its suffering multitudes, it carried them all in its heart on the road to the Golgothian peak. It staggered and groaned under the weight of the foreign yoke, but no humble Cyrenaic came to lighten its load. It sweated blood and tears, but no sweet Veronica came to wipe its forehead with her scarf. All around it, mounds of mute stone, but no friendly shoulder. All around, harshness and brute force, but not one iota of gentleness or a glimmer of joy – not even in sleeping. The night was as ong as a sorrow and the longed-for dawn far beyond nine mountains. Only evangelic faith and hope sustained the weary and consoled the wretched sufferers.

In the 19th century and buttressed by the love they bore for their long--suffering homeland, the Franciscans made their way into their forsaken Herzegovina and, beneath the open skies and an ancient oak on Široki Brijeg, they laid the foundations of a new Herzegovian Franciscan Order. Soon afterwards and following almost 300 years of utter desolation, the first churches and monasteries rose in Herzegovian as glowing beacons of centres of spirituality and as glittering sources of culture and civilization for the benefit of God's church and God's people. Sadly though, Herzegovina was not fated to enjoy a long spell of this new ambience and grace. Soon, the terrifying winds of two world wars were to sweep through, whipping up a sea of innocent human blood and rivers of bitter human tears. And in the cradle of the Herzegovian Franciscan Order, on Široki Brijeg, the blood of numerous Franciscan friars was shed. But out of that blood and that carnage the Herzegovian Church was to grow again, this time with an energy and a flowering the like of which had not been seen before. Then came new tribulations and suffering: a controversy arose between the diocesan clergy and the Franciscans regarding a new division of the dioceses, which became known as the Herzegovian Church Case. And amid this confict, unsettled to this day, and flood of unbelievable grace rose in Medugorje which has attracted the eyes of the world.

The old Herzegovian chronicler, Fra Petar Bakula, recorded 120 years ago that many people had made frequent claims of having seen a very strong red light, and who said that they were convinced that the light revealed some great treasure. Were not the ancient seers of Medugorje true and real prophets when they claimed that the light revealed hidden treasure? Is there any greater treasure from merciful Heaven than that which today in Medugorje is bestowing its kisses on this Earth? Are there more priceless riches to be obtained than the Heavenly Mother Mary being a friend to all her earthly children? ■

Dr Ljudevit Rupčić

TODAY

This is the moment of truth. Dreams of paradise on Earth are being transformed into apocalyptic reality. Ideologies are already reaping a bitter harvest. Human efforts are ending in failure. Prospects are becoming ever more bleak. Everything that has occurred is quite contrary to what was declared, promised and planned. United nations have become disjointed nations. Advanced nations have developed the material but have retarded man. The backward are doing their utmost to catch up with and even overtake them in that regard. The free have become fast and wild and the unfree in their pursuit of freedom have taken the path of terrorism.

The lie is being preached as the truth; crimes are being perpetrated in the name of justice; slavery is being bolstered in the name of freedom. In the name of a people, human rights are the name of freedom. In the name of a people, human rights are being violated. In the name of a brighter future, the present is being stolen. Democrats, anti-democrats, racists and humanists differ greatly one from the other – in their utterances. The less they are willing of able to do the more they promise. They fail to fulfil their promises. Shunning the present by escaping into the future they proceed from bad to worse.

Words have come to lose their substance and now mean quite the contrary. Meaning has been ejected from life; love from the heart; morality from politics; responsibility from actions.

All values have been reduced to material interests and morals to the skill of satisfying them. Man has become the currency with which both success and failure are paid for.

Social structures are the chains which bind lamenting man. Power has become an end in itself. It does not serve the ends of man, rather it is he who is in its service. Instead of making itself superfluous and unnecessary it makes man supernumerary by turning him into redundant jetsam. The manner in which it flourishes under totalitarianism highlights the fact that uncontrolled power equates to anarchy and tyranny. Through it, people learn how to become inhuman; whereas the weaker, oppressed by its yoke, can be but the accused, never the judges.

PEACE is something merely dreamt of by humanity; its realities are wars, social injustices, unemployment, terrorism, AIDS and hopelessness. The human alternative to PEACE is the peace of the powerless, the deprived and the downtrodden. This is a peace worse than war; for war kills the armed, while a peace such as this such destroys the unarmed. Where the flames of war are not burning, this peace is raging. A state has been reached where it is increasingly difficult to refute the claim made by the 17th-century English philosopher, Thomas Hobbes, that war by all against all is a natural state.

The Earth has become a killing ground for man; progress his execution with history ensuring its perpetuity.

This is the moment of opportunity. In spite of all that has happened the world is not void of paradoxical hope and opportunity. This is parenthetically linked to Međugorje, but fundamentally to what has been said there and to what is occurring there. The authentic testimony of millions of people; uncountable representatives of all social and cultural profiles; contrasting concepts of the world; various races, classes and ages, guarantee that peace is being experienced in a different manner, on a different path and with different means than has been the case until now. They have found it by following the way indicated by Our Lady – through faith, conversion and by prayer. And that peace is God Himself, who is "our peace in Christ" (Ephes 2:14).

The battlefield for peace is man's heart, the source of hatred, injustice, wars, "murders" (Mat 15:19), "craftiness and mindlessness" (Mark 7:22) and every other evil. Such is the human heart. And so it shall stay until it is converted. If the roots of all evils are not wrenched from the heart through conversion then they will continue their unrestrained growth, feeding increasingly poisonous fruits. Any other course that may be taken would be a despairing and injurious failure. "The world is not changed from without, but from within" (L. Tolstoy).

April 25, 1987

Dear children! Today also I am calling you to prayer. You know, dear children, that God grants special grace in prayer. Therefore, seek and pray in order that you may be able to comprehend all that I am giving here. I call you, dear children, to prayer with the heart. You know that without prayer you cannot comprehend all that God is planning throughd each one of you. Therefore, pray! I desire that through each one of you God's plan may be fulfilled, that all which God has planted in your heart may keep on growing. So pray that God's blessing may protect each one of you from all the evil that is threatening you. I bless you, dear children. Thank you for having responded to my call.

Peace does not follow in the wake of victorious armies but of converted sinners. All people are sinners; the most insidious among them being those who will not admit to it and who refuse to convert. Despite all their endeavours at "peace making" they are but arsonists in fireman's clothing.

In Međugorje, people do not settle accounts with others but with themselves. They do not point a besmirched finger at others, but at themselves. Their precious contribution to peace is their own reorientation towards values that are permanent and immutable – towards God and love. Only through the conversion of all shall total and all pervading peace be established. And to that there is no other road. All else is merely the blood soaked path to a mockery of peace.

New United Nations are being created in Međugorje which do not discuss peace; rather they are winning it and living it through conversion. Their interest lies with love through deeds and not through shallow discussions about it. They enrich themselves through others while their mutual differences draw them closer together. Their problems, remedies, joys and sorrows are common. They have waged war on war, hunger, injustice and misery, and not on man. A crime aginst one man is a crime against the whole of humanity. Other people are not hell, as Sartre has said they are, but they are brothers, as Jesus Christ has said they are.

They are those who have stepped from a lost past into the future. They are, contrary to those ideological tellers of fortunes, the authentic witnesses of a brighter future. In having come from it they offer irrefutable testimony of the new strength, the new road and the new beginning.

This is the moment of decision. The Mother of God, who is also our mother, brings the gladdening news to us and to the whole world – the gates of heaven are open to us. God wants to meet us and to make a gift of Himself to us in Christ, of His life, His strength, His future and His destiny.

What now can there be that is so important and needed than the coming together with Christ that His mother has presented to us?

In the words of Gerhard Tersteegen:

"God is still calling
Should I not finally come?
'Twas not so long ago I heard the faithful voice
I know so well: I have not been what I should have been;
He beckoned to me but I refused to know him.
God still calls, have I stopped my ears;
He still stands at my door, knocking;
He is still prepared to receive me;
He ist still waiting for me. Who knows for how long?« ■

Fra Svetozar Kraljević

A JOURNEY TO AFRICA

If it is possible for one to compare small things with large then I can say that my journey into Africa made the pain, effort and sacrifice borne by the Holy Father during His pastoral wanderings through the world abundantly clear to me. Great physical and mental efforts, encounters with peoples and lands and their sufferings and trials, the vast distances from all that represents the security and safety of one's home – all this provided just a glimmer of the life of a pilgrim, the way of life of the outcast, of a life shadowed by the ordeal of Calvary. It helped me understand better than ever the magnitude of the missionary calling and the courage of those who dare to tread this road of sacrifice and self-denial.

There was something of a missionary Christian symbolism even in the departure itself. Those things that should have come from Dubrovnik to Rome were never to arrive – apart from documents, which I carried with me anyway. In Lusaka and Harare my hosts were given a opportunity to display the depths of their charitableness by providing me with a habit and everything else necessary, while I was unable to respond to their gesture – not even with a medal.

The Reverend Doctor Ivan Cerovac SJ met me at the airport. During the few days I was to spend with him he altered a few of the ideas I had harboured about the priest's calling. Through him I learned that there are priests who have selflessly and courageously surrendered themselves to a life of exacting self-denial. His meagre African diet, his humble home, his ministrations to the sick, his unsparing assistance to and involvement with the faithful no matter what they asked of him, his long drives to distant missions among the lepers and the brutally poor, all revealed to me the qualities demanded by a priestly life that are seen ever more rarely. Hew took me to the Archbishop of Lusaka who had just returned from a long journey to quite the opposite part of the land. A great man behind a simple demeanour. The encounter with him offered at one and the same time an experience of Rome and of Africa, of discipline and of Fatherhood. I possessed just one rosary which I wanted to present to him, but he refused to accept it unless I took his own in order that I could also pray.

In Lusaka I spoke to a large gathering of people. Most of them were black. And although I will never be sure whether my thoughts penetrated their reason I did perceive, stronger than ever before, that love is the only way of communicating and that within it everything is crystal clear – even when words take us nowhere. I prayed that God may speak to them without me. Priests told me of their own prayers and hopes for a sanctuary of the Blessed Virgin Mary, the Queen of Peace, to be built close to Lusaka.

My visit to Zimbabwe was a brief one and my impressions of that country are undefined. I was not able to properly understand whether this was a country of whites or blacks, rich or poor, modern and industrialized, or one belonging to the third world. Maybe that is why it could serve as a model for some fresh thoughts about life in Africa, so parched and thirsting for the words of God. Poor Clares in Harare seem to have embodied the fate of faith of the country. Like jewels they share the lustre of their lives with people who appear to take them as an adornment, but without wishing to share in the glory. The Poor Clares arrived in Zimbabwe from Spain and like some beautiful adornment they await the moment when some local girl assumes herself the same lustre.

At the airport in Lilongwe, the capital of Malawi, I was met by Mme Gay Russell, a pilot, great friend and propagator of the messages of Our Lady of Medugorje. About one hundred followers who were with her greeted me with singing and dancing. The aircraft was put at our disposal for seven days and we were thus able to visit all the major centres around the country. Malawai – a poor, misery-filled land taking its first, faltering steps into the civilization of today. During his pastoral visit the Holy Father asked the Jesuit Fathers to take over the local school of theology and to inspire it with a new spirit and a new ecclesiastical quality.

In the north, in Karonga, I met a young priest (I trust he will forgive me for having forgotten his name) who embodies all the best that the Church desires to give to Africa. Looking at him, I said to myself: *This is what Malawi needs* – faith, discipline in work, knowledge, modesty and optimism. Just at that time a home for the young was in the process of construction. The unemployed young can be numbered in their thousands. This priest has himself organized the production of baked bricks as well as everything else. Having begun with no money whatsoever he has put his faith firmly in God's providence. And he believes that the Church is becoming the symbol of hope for his so very poor flock. Active togetherness in the liturgy and in physical labour is what the Church is seeking in Africa. In a parish so far removed and where everything is so fundamentally different from the world I come from, it was a source of wonder to see a group of believers who call themselves *The Friends of Medugorje*. They pray regularly and take it upon themselves to be friends and the bearers of peace; noble Christians. They pray every day; on Fridays they join together in communal prayer and on Sundays they regularly attend Holy Mass. Their acts are acts of love and grace. By the time I was due to leave a strong impression had grown in my mind: If this country were to have a few thousand new, devoted and holy priests, engineers, economists, administrators, doctors, etc., who could combine their expertise with love, the country would burgeon with a new life. They told me that AIDS is stalking Africa like a roaring, perpetually hungry lion looking for his next victim.

The Republic of South Africa – a revelation of wealth and glitter, but also of a human thirst for truth and peace. Thousands listened to my words. I told them that through conversion to God, to prayer, acts of mercy and through active participation in the life of the Church, they could discover within themselves the person that God had wanted from the beginning and thus return to the full realization of the sense of their own living. God offers Himself to man as a small and helpless child so that man will receive Him, bring Him up, take care of Him, give Him love and kindness. Abortion is first and foremost a state of human spirit in which the fragile flutterings of faith are mercilessly stilled and swept away by the onslaught of world opinion. Within a body the aborting of an unborn child is the most dramatic expression of the aggressive condition of the human spirit.

How much more I would have to write if I were to relate everything about my encounters with those believers in Lilongwe Cathedral; about the unbelievably well-disciplined children; about the singing that seemed to emanate from another world; about the man who came to the church barefooted, who has six children, makes his living raising corn – and who is happy; about John Bradburn and the lepers in Mutemwa; about the faithful in Katete; about Dr John Mwalula; about the magical power of God's world spoken and witnessed through a woman's life of suffering in South Africa; about Dr Tony Manning; about Bishops and Archbishops whom I met, and about so many other wonderful signs of a God continually giving Himself to man in his everyday life.

Fra Veselko Grubišić and Fra Marijan Zlovečera made it possible for me to meet the Croatian community in Johannesburg. They have just started on the construction of a new and beautiful church. Parents of the families who come here from Croatian regions count their tears, while their children retain dim memories of their distant land and of a people they are told so much about. I am not sure that the material wealth they have gained will console them for all they have left behind them.

Apart from bringing home to me the sharp realization that man is but a passer-by, a pilgrim on this Earth, my journey to Africa has taught me that man has no other way of fulfilling himself other than through God. That is patently clear in a man of Africa, be he black or white. The white man, however long he may live in Africa and however deep his roots have penetrated, remains forever a stranger from another world. The black man – poor, sick, short-lived, out of harmony with nature and himself, badly hurt by the new steps taken by civilization, remains a stranger to life itself. Through his life of suffering the African is nailed to the cross of his own homeland. With all that in mind, the words of St Paul to the Corinthians come to mind: "We are confident, I say, and willing to be absent from the body, and to be present with the Lord." (2 Cor. 5:8).

At the end of my journey there was another thought which would not leave my mind: The hands of the Blessed Virgin Mary of Medugorje have reached deeply and far into the very being of the Church. This is the Medugorje that encourages and binds, that has to be known and respected. And it binds the priests of the Church in a special way; it binds them to stay alert and to transmit this pure message that the world is awaiting like some arid desert waits for rain. ■

April 25, 1988

Dear children! God wants to make you holy. Therefore, through me He is calling you to complete surrender. Let the Holy Mass be your life. Understand that the church is God's palace, the place in which I gather you and want to show you the way to God. Come and pray! Neither look to others nor slander them, but rather let your life be a testimony on the way of holiness. Churches deserve respect and are set apart as holy because God, who became Man, dwells in them day and night. Therefore, little children, believe and pray that the Father increase your faith, and then ask for whatever you need. I am with you and I rejoice because of your conversion and I am protecting you with my motherly mantle. Thank you for having responded to my call.

March 25, 1988

Dear children! Today also I am calling you to a complete surrender to God. You, dear children, are not conscious of how God loves you with such a great love. Because of it He permits me to be with you so I can instruct you and help you to find the way of peace. That way, however, you cannot discover if you do not pray. Therefore, dear children, forsake everything and consecrate your time to God and then God will bestow gifts upon you and bless you. Little children, do not forget that your life is fleeting like the spring flower which today is wondrously beautiful, but tomorrow has vanished. Therefore, pray in such a way that your prayer, your surrender to God may become like a road sign. That way your witness will not only have value for yourselves, but for all of eternity. Thank you for having responded to my call.

Georg W. Kosicki, C.S.B.

CONSECRATION: A WAY OF LIFE

Consecration to Jesus through Mary is a way of life. It is an Eucharistic consecration, and in the words of the Holy Father, it is a "total gift, a total yes, *Totus Tuus.*"

I'd like to start with some witnesses and I'll start with myself. I know the importance, the value, the power and the necessity of consecration now, but it was not that way all the time. Back in 1946, I found a book called *True Devotion to the Blessed Virgin Mary*, by St. Louis de Monfort. I was fascinated by it, and yet at the same time, kind of fearful. What's this slavery to Mary? What is Mary going to do? Is she going to take me away from Jesus? Is she an obstacle to Jesus? I was fearful and I did not make the consecration at that time. It wasn't till April 23, the Feast of St. George in 1970, that in the Church of my baptism, at the statue of the Pieta, Mary holding Jesus, I experienced a deliverance of fear of giving myself to Mary. It was an important moment for me. Later, during the Ignatian exercises, at the end of each of the many hours of prayer, I said, "Mary, how can I do this?" "Just take my hand and walk as a child, as a son of God, walk in the light", seemed to be her response. In 1975 I again committed myself unconditionally as a slave of Mary, and things began to open up for me.

Let us look at the witness of Pope John Paul II. His motto is *"Totus Tuus"*, I'm all yours, Mary. And what does John Paul say about that? He says, "I'm not ashamed of being a slave of Mary because this means the fullness of liberty and dignity, a freedom that makes us truly free." He says, "It's a holy slavery of our baptism and our consecration to Jesus through Mary is an absolute entrustment to Jesus. It's giving one's self entirely to Mary in order to belong wholly to Jesus through her."

What is the meaning of that consecration for John Paul? For him it means that what Jesus has done for us as priest and victim, we individually and corporately, must ratify, appropriate, and make our own by entrusting ourselves to Mary. That means accepting her help as mother and model to go to the source of our salvation, to the foundation of mercy, to the cross. Pope John Paul says in doing this, we consecrate the world to the Father, which means we bring the world to the fount of mercy, to the pierced side of Jesus, to the Sacred Heart today.

We are speaking of a consecration to Jesus through Mary as a way of life. Let's take a look at each of these phrases.

What is "consecration"? The word means to make holy, to sacrifice, to set aside as special gift as holy to be offered, to be totally given, total yes, *Totus Tuus.* For Christians, this total yes is to Christ. It is a total yes to his gift as we are baptized into Christ with the fullness of initiation into his body. The word "baptism" in scripture includes the whole of our initiation, which includes the sacrament of baptism in water, confirmation, and Holy Eucharist. There is one baptism, one whole and total initiation into Christ that includes the three sacraments, and consecration is a total yes to this whole baptism. It is threefold.

Consecration is a yes to the baptims of water, dying to self in order to rise in Christ, to being alive for Him alone, to be children of the Father, to be a children of Mary, to join His family, rejecting sin, and rejecting Satan.

Consecration is also a total yes to the Holy Spirit, a surrender, a yielding, an abandonment, a yes to being possessed by the Spirit that we may be used by Him, yes to His power, yes to His gifts, yes to His fruit!

Consecration is also yes to Eucharist, a total yes to Christ, to be His body, His blood, broken and poured out, to be total gift, to be humble, to be consumed, to be given.

And so, consecration is to *be Eucharist,* the body and blood of Christ for the sake of the world, channels of mercy to bring forgiveness and salvation to all. That is what consecration is, a total yes.

Now, why to Jesus? Jesus is the way to the Father. Jesus is the yes to the Father. Jesus reveals the Father and his mercy and is transparent to the Father. Seeing Jesus, we see the Father. We imitate Jesus in His own threefold consecration. The Father consecrated his son on coming into the world (John 10:36). Jesus consecrated himself (John 17:19), and Jesus consecrates us (John 17:17).

But why through Mary? Why? Because this is the way Jesus did it. Jesus came to us born of Mary in the Spirit. In Matthew 1:30, and again in Luke 1:35, the Word was given uniquely to Mary and to nobody else. Jesus submitted Himself to Mary in the temple. He set His priorities on the Father and then in obedience submitted Himself to Mary and to Joseph (Luke 2:51), and then Jesus gave Mary to us (John 19:25–27). Jesus submitted Himself to Mary and who am I not to imitate Jesus?

"Jesus was conceived and born in Mary's womb by the Spirit" (Creed). We too are born of Mary and the Spirit (Acts 1:14). She is our mother. That's baptism! In the Cenacle, waiting for the Spirit, she taught the apostles and disciples how to surrender to the Spirit. That's her special gift, the total unconditional surrender to the Spirit to be used to bring forth incarnate mercy, Jesus Christ. We too are taught like the Apostles to surrender. Mary's role in the Eucharist is to bring us to the source of the Eucharist, to the cross of Jesus. She was commissioned at the cross in the great statement, "Woman, behold your son", which is another way of Jesus' saying to her, "Woman, this is My Body. Woman, this is Eucharist."

And so why consecration to Mary? Because, we imitate Jesus who came through Mary. We go the way He came. We go to the cross of jesus to be Eucharist. Consecration to Jesus means to allow Mary to take us to the cross of Jesus in order to be Eucharist. Consecration to Mary is an Eucharistic consecration, which then becomes a way of life, that God may be all in all to bring all things in one in Christ.

What does it mean to be Eucharist? I would suggest one way of understanding that, is to look at Jesus in the Eucharist. Look at the host, look at it carefully. You seek bread, but with the eyes of faith, you see radiant light. Listen to that host, what do you hear? Nothing... silence. The mystic, Sister Faustina said, "God has a language of His own and He speaks powerfully and loudly, but that language is silence" (Diary 888). Approach Jesus with your touch in your hand or the touch of your tongue. What do you feel? Bread? But, with a touch of faith it is a fire of divine love. Approach the host with your heart and you will see Jesus meek and humble of hearts, totally given, a total yes, a total surrender, transformed by the Spirit, consecrated, a channel of mercy to us all. He says, "Take and eat." We become what we eat. We become more and more the Body of Christ. You say, "Well I look the same." But with the eyes of faith you radiate in a different way. And so we live the Eucharist by living daily our whole initiation into Christ, our baptism, our confirmation, and our Eucharist. And so, *Totus Tuus*, consecration to Jesus through Mary is a way of life. It is to be and to live the Eucharist.

We are entering into a very spacial time, a time of preparation for the new millennium, the two thousandth year of Christianity. We began this preparation in a special way with the Marian year, entering into what the Holy Father has called a Marian Advent, preparing for this mystic time of the year 2000. In this time especially, it is Mary's role to prepare the Bride, the Chruch, you and me, that the Bride together with the Spirit may say, "Come, Lord Jesus." If we really are united as the Bride of Christ, as Eucharist, with the Spirit, together crying, "Come, Lord Jesus." He will be here in a new radiance and we will have a new Eucharistic Church.

To begin to live this consecration to Jesus through Mary, to live Eucharistically our lives, to prepare for this new millenium, pray daily the following prayer of Consecration:

> *"Mary, Mother of Jesus, and Mother of Mercy,*
> *since Jesus from the cross gave you to me,*
> *I take you as my own.*
> *And since Jesus gave me to you,*
> *take me as your own.*
> *Make me docile like Jesus on the cross,*
> *obedient to the Father, trusting in humility and in love.*
> *Mary, my Mother,*
> *in imitation of the Father who gave His son,*
> *I give my all to you.*
> *To you I entrust all that I am, all that I have, and all that I do.*
> *Help me to surrender ever more fully to the Spirit,*
> *lead me deeper into the mystery of the cross,*
> *the cenacle, and the fullness of Church.*
> *As your formed the Heart of Jesus by the Spirit,*
> *form my heart to be the throne of Jesus in His glorious coming.*
> *Amen.* ∎

September 25, 1987

Dear children! Today also I want to call you all to prayer. Let prayer be your life. Dear children, dedicate your time only to Jesus and He will give you everything that you are seeking. He will reveal Himself to you in fulness. Dear children, Satan is strong and is waiting to test each one of you. Pray, and that way he will neither be able to injure you nor block you on the way of holiness. Dear children, through prayer grow all the mores toward God from day to day. Thank you for having responded to my call.

Dr Mark Miravalle

"CONSECRATE YOURSELVES TOTALLY TO MY IMMACULATE HEART..."

The most complete ancient prayer to the Blessed Virgin Mary that has survived from the days of the early Church is the *Sub Tuum Praesidium* (litterally, "Under Your Protection"):

We fly to your patronage, O Holy Mother of God,
despise not our petitions in our necessities,
but deliver us from all dangers,
O glorious and blessed Virgin. (C. 250 AD)

How beautiful was this filial call of the third century faithful to the Mother of Jesus for protection and deliverance! How profound was their understanding of Mary as a spiritual mother who, like no other, had the ability to intercede to our Lord for the most fundamental spiritual and physical needs of her earthly children!

Can we say today that the members of the Mystical Body of Jesus, in our own age, have the same penetrating understanding of the need to "fly to the patronage" of the Mother of God? Do we, as the people of God today grasp the importance of giving ourselves to Mary in the midst of the immense spiritual and physical dangers that threaten the life and well-being of the Church and the modern world?

There are at least two contemporary voices which are calling us to entrust ourselves to the "special protection" that comes to us from the Blessed Virgin Mary, who is the "Help of Christians" and "Mother of the Church".

The first contemporary voice is, appropriately so, the Blessed Virgin herself.

From the remote Yugoslavian mountain town called Međugorje, the Queen of Peace is inviting the world to consecrate themselves to her Immaculate Heart, that sanctuary of maternal love and God-given channel to the Sacred Heart of Jesus.

"Consecrate yourselves to my Immaculate Heart. Abandon yourselves totally. I will protect you." This sublime invitation of Mary to give ourselves completely to her hints at the ultimate goal of such Marian consecration: to receive that spiritual protection and ever greater union with Jesus Christ, which the Father would like each and every person to receive. The Father has seen it fit to make this spiritual gift available to us through the same channel by which we received our Lord Jesus Himself – the person of Mary.

The Madonna of Međugorje also summons us to consecrate our families daily to the Sacred Heart of Jesus and has revealed specific prayers of consecration to the Sacred Heart of Jesus and the Immaculate Heart of Mary which were given to Jelena Vasilj in 1983. The prayer of consecration to the Immaculate Heart begins simply, but profoundly:

O my Mother,
Mother of goodness, of love and mercy,
I love you infinitely,
and I offer myself to you.

The second contemporary voice inviting the world to entrust themselves to the Mother of God is that of Pope John Paul II. Both in word and in deed, the Holy Father is calling the world to give themselves to this unique care of Mary.

On March 25, 1984, Pope John Paul II, along with many bishops throughout the world, consecrated the world to the Immaculate Heart of Mary, amidst the tears and cheers of well over a half million faithful in St. Peter's square. And in his recent Marian encyclical, *Redemptoris Mater,* Mother of the Redeemer, which called for the commencement of the 1987 Marian year, the Pope presents a beautiful theology of Marian consecration which he refers to as a "filial entrustment to the Mother of Christ".

In this theology of consecration to Mary, the Holy Father directs our gaze to the foot of the Cross (Jn. 19:26). It is here at Calvary that Jesus gave Mary as Spiritual Mother to John, who is a symbol of all who seek to be "beloved disciples". The Pope states: "Mary's motherhood, which becomes man's inheritance, is a gift: a gift which Christ himself makes personally to every individual" (*Redemptoris Mater,* No. 45).

The call of Jesus at Calvary to "behold the Mother" is a summons of Christ to every Christian disciple. We should note that the words of our Saviour are not in the form of an invitation. He does not say, "Would you like to take my Mother as your Mother?" Our crucified Lord rather states the theological and spiritual truth of Mary's spiritual motherhood, and then calls us to "behold" our newly given Mother.

Our question then becomes, how precisely should we behold Mary as Spiritual Mother? How should the Christian disciple practically respond to this gift of Mary, a gift given to us personally by Jesus himself? Let us learn from the example given by John the beloved disciple.

The Gospel records John's response: "And from that hour, the disciple took her into his own home" (Jn. 19:27). John brings Mary into his own home, and so too should every disciple of Christ. According to our Holy Father, the special way in which we invite Mary "into our homes" is by offering ourselves as spiritual sons and daughters to our Mother.

"The Marian dimension of the life of a disciple of Christ is expressed in a special way precisely through this filial entrusting to the Mother of Christ... Entrusting himself to Mary in a filial manner, the Christian, like the Apostle John, "welcomes the Mother of Christ into his own home" (*Redemptoris Mater*, No. 45).

The word, "home", John Paul II explains, is the inner life, the spiritual life of the believer. When we welcome Mary into our spiritual lives, we allow our Mother to use her unique power of intercession to lead us ever closer to a profound living in and with Christ and his Body the Church. The more we give of ourselves to this Mother, the more she is made free to, moment by moment, guide us in becoming transformed in grace and being true to our baptismal promises. When we entrust ourselves to Mary, we allow her to do what is a principal concern of every mother: to unite her children. Ultimately, Mary's task is to unite interiorly and perpetually her earthly children throughout the world with Him who is her First Child, instructing all of humanity daily to "do whatever He tells you" (Jn. 2:5).

The Pope also calls us in this Marian encyclical to appreciate the rich Marian spirituality of St. Louis Marie de Montfort who proposes "consecration to Christ through the hands of Mary as an effective means for Christians to live faithfully their baptismal promises" (*Redemptoris Mater*, No. 48). The ultimate goal of Marian consecration is always a greater fidelity to the life of grace in Jesus Christ through the help of her whom Vatican II proclaimed as our "mother in the order of grace".

It is noteworthy that Pope John Paul II personally consecrates himself each day to the Mother of Jesus using de Montfort's long form of Marian consecration. Furthermore, John Paul's papal motto, *Totus Tuus,* comes from the first two words of de Montfort's short consecration to Mary which is translated, "completely and entirely yours".

Let us then heed the wisdom of the early Church and the contemporary voice of Pope John Paul II as echoed by the Madonna of Medugorje in her October 25, 1988 message to the world:

Dear children! My call that you live the messages which I am giving you is a daily one. Especially, little children, because I want to draw you closer to the Heart of Jesus. Therefore, little children, I am calling you today to the prayer of Consecration to Jesus, my dear Son, so that each of your hearts may be His. And then I am calling you to Consecration to my Immaculate Heart. I want you to consecrate yourselves as persons, families and parishes so that all belongs to God through my hands. Therefore, dear little children, pray that you may comprehend the greatness of this message which I am giving you. I do not want anything for myself, rather all for the salvation of your souls. Satan is strong and, therefore, you little children, by constant prayer, press tightly to my motherly heart. Thank you for having responded to my call.

Let us formally offer ourselves to the special protection of the Mother of God in this age of such severe and ubiquitous spiritual impoverishment. Let us avail ourselves of this efficacious means of receiving the spiritual peace of Jesus Christ in our hearts through Mary, Queen of Peace.

I conclude wiht a modern Marian prayer of protection and consecration, written by Pope John Paul II during the 1983 Holy Year of Redemption and specifically intended for use by Christian families:

Most Holy Virgin, Mother of God and of the Church,
to your Immaculate Heart we today consecrate our family.

With your help, we entrust and consecrate
ourselves to the Divine Heart of Jesus;

In order to be with you and with Him
in the Holy Spirit;

Completely and always entrusted and consecrated to
the will of the Heavenly Father.

Amen. ■

Zlata Vucelić

IN VASILJI

■ Jelena's Little Sister and Grandmother

■ Jelena Vasilj

MARY, MY HEAVENLY MOTHER

I have to be quite honest when I say I didn't know a lot about Mother Mary until my pilgrimage to Međugorje in the Spring of 1986. At best, I would say some fleeting prayer to her and, if I had time, I'd say the Rosary. I never really understood what it meant to have a heavenly Mother; a heavenly Mother who cares so much that she willingly and consistently approaches the throne of God asking Him to bestow good things on His children; a mother so patient and kind that she wants to teach and lead me to a closer relationship with her Son, Jesus Christ.

I remember looking forward to the journey, hoping that I, too, would see a great sign or wonder. The Lord had different plans, though. He wanted me to testify to miracles, not physical but rather spiritual; a miracle of the heart, a miracle that called me to a deeper conversion, a deeper faith and trust, and a deeper love of service.

One miracle of the heart occurred on Mt. Krizevac, the hill of the Cross. Atop the biggest hill in Međugorje sits a thirty foot cement cross. Pilgrims climb the mountain daily to pray the Stations of te Cross which dot the path leading to the cross and then to pray at the foot of the Cross when they arive at the top.

I decided, as a penance, to walk up the mountain in my bare feet. As I began my climb and proceeded to the first station, there were many sharp rocks and it was hard to pick my way among them. I found myself whimpering in pain from the sharp rocks. Yet, as I looked around, crippled people and old people uncomplainingly climbed the mountain. I was amazed at their dedication and strength. Then I thought of Our Lord. He was flogged, slapped, beaten, mocked, spat upon, and then mercilessly left to hang until death on a cross — al because He loved me. Jesus held nothing back. He allowed Himself to be vulnerable to those who hated Him and they killed Him.

My heart then broke and I cried and asked the Lord to forgive me. What was my pain compared to His? I realized that even if I had been the only one left in the world, Christ still would have died for me. But then, I also would have killed Him. At that moment, I knew the incredible love of the Lord and the least I could do would be to finish climbing.

God in His beautiful mercy instilled in me an understanding that the way of the cross is love. I rejoice that I, too, can share in Christ's passion.

Before my trip to Međugorje, I can best describe myself as fearful. Fear had a grip on my life that kept me from reaching out to others. I was afraid to be vulnerable to others because I didn't want to be hurt, a very human characteristic. But the fear was so great that I would have nightmares that literally would leave me paralyzed with fear until I would fall asleep an hour or two later.

One night, during the pilgrimage, I was overcome with this deep fear. I called out to my roommates to pray with me. As they prayed with me, they asked Mother Mary's protection and slowly the fear fell away and in its place, I felt the comforting arms of my heavenly Mother.

Since that night, I have experienced a tremendous release from fear and I am now able to put my trust in Jesus and Mary, and to step out and serve others.

One way that I constantly have to trust the Lord is in my pro-life work. Presently, I rescue* full-time. For me, rescue is a manifestation of what I learned in Međugorje. Every time I am arrested, I am allowing myself to be vulnerable to a system that sometimes is unjust. I can only surrender to Jesus, though. The Lord asks me to live as He lived, to follow the way of the cross and to surrender everything to Him. Sometimes it is very hard and many times I fail, but my one comfort is that I have a Mother in heaven who is praying for me.

Susan Ferguson
Steubenville, Ohio

* Rescue is an international effort to block entrance to abortion clinics, in order to rescue babies from being murdered. ■

MEĐUGORJE INFLUENCE ON MOTHER

Mother seemed at the point of death from a cancerous tumor that blocked her esophagus. I traveled home to St. Augustine, Florida for a few days to visit her in the hospital before she died. She rallied and we took her home. Soon after I had returned to Steubenville, my father was hospitalized with back pain from the tension of having to cope with the total care of mother alone. When I called home I learned that mother had not even had a glass of water so far that day because no one was available and she was took weak to get up alone. The next day I was on my way back to Florida. The following three weeks a very special, grace-filled gift from God for my family.

For the first three days, I juggled between hospital visits and caring for mother. Then it was between physical therapy for dad and decisions about more radiation or intravenous feeding for mother. Questions about hospice care or other available support had to be explored. In the meantime the tumor would obstruct food and sometimes, even the saliva from entering mother's stomach. She would gag and vomit. Often it would happen at night and so I "slept" in the room with mother. At one point mother needed me but I had no energy to get up. Suddenly the room was filled with light and I felt supportive strength carry me to her side. The next day I told my dad about my experience. It was about the same time that night that dad had felt the Holy Spirit told him to tell mother that it was all right for her to die; that God wanted her with Him; that He would provide for my dad. For the next week and a half dad struggled to be able to tell her, but didn't, even though there seemed to be several opportunities.

In spite of all of this mother bravely fought to live. On one of her better evenings we watched a video on Mary's apparitions in Međugorje. After seeing the video, Mother grew very quiet and only wanted to be helped to bed. The next morning the first thing mother said to me was, "On the video we watched last night, Mary said we need to be reconciled. Help me to my chair and bring me my pen and stationery. I have something to do". She wrote the last letter of her life to her brother from whom she had been estranged for 40 years, asking to be reconciled. Two nights later we watched the same video again and a similar quiet overtook mother. The next morning she questioned me about Mary's message of forgiveness. Mother was concerned about how she could forgive someone who had hurt her deeply many years before. I encouraged her to pray and ask God to give her His ability to forgive with an openness in her heart to do whatever He guided her to do beyond that. She prayed and became very peaceful.

Several nights later mother begged to be taken to the emergency room as she was gagging so badly. They admitted her where she spent the last week of her life. The first couple days she would say to daddy and me, "I'll fight this thing. I'll be home again soon." Over Friday night she must have had an encounter with God because Saturday morning she greeted us with, "I'm going to die soon." At that point daddy finally had the grace to follow through with what he knew the Holy Spirit had inspired him to do and released her. She asked for Father Baker, her pastor. We notified my brothers and sisters who began arriving. A cot was brought to the room for me to stay with mother. All day as mother drifted in and out of sleep she began the process of putting the last tasks in order. She even asked me to finish some of her knitting projects. Each time she woke up, she started where she left off. Saturday night her youngest son arrived. My brother was able to tell her that he had seen the priest the night before and was able to receive the sacraments again. There was a joy on her face that said, "All I have suffered is worth it"

Sunday morning when she woke up she looked at me and said, "Oh, I'm still here. I thought I would be with Jesus." When Father Baker came again that afternoon she told him, "Mary didn't come yet to take me to Jesus." She imagined Mary would take her into her arms like she held Jesus in the "Pieta" and present her to her Son. Those were among her last words even though she lingered on for several days. One night she was not turned every two hours as ordered and by morning her back was a mass of bruises and bed sores. When I saw it, my first reaction was a deep awareness of the scourging Jesus endured. From that moment Jesus' suffering became real to me. I knew my mother's pain. I saw it in her eyes and on her face, even though she couldn't talk. Now I know the pain that Jesus endured, for our sins cause him real pain. Jesus had been a statue or a ceramic crucifix to me before. Now I know He suffered and felt the pain as a real human person.

Through the video, Mary's message from Medugorje touched my mother to help prepare her for the death. She responded to the need for reconciliation with her brother and to forgiveness in another relationship. She faced her death courageously and peacefully, waiting for Mary to take her to Jesus. And for me, I now know Jesus in a way that was not real before. Mary's March 6, 1986 message took on new meaning for me:

Dear Children: Today I call you to open yourselves more to God, so that He can work through you. The more you open yourselves, the more you receive the fruits. I wish to call you again to prayer. Thank you for having responded to my call. ■

Harriet Hrezo
Steubenville, Ohio

I had multiple sclerosis for twenty-six years, with the last seven of those years being extremely difficult. The multiple sclerosis became increasingly worse, causing complete paralysis of my feet and ankles and structural deformities of my legs. My knees were turned inward. The right leg was especially bad. I was allowed to "walk" short distances when at home, in the house, with the aid of full length leg braces and forearm crutches. But most of the day I spent in a wheel chair.

I had just gone to bed on Wednesday June 18, 1986, having finished my daily rosary, when the sudden thought came to me to ask Jesus, through the intercession of Our Lady of Medugorje, for a cure. Recently, I had read about Mary's appearances at Medugorje in several Catholic periodicals and I had just finished Father Rene Laurentin's book, "Is the Virgin Mary Appearing at Medugorje?" In response to Our Mother's request, I had begun to fast several days a week. I had never prayed for a cure before. My prayer was only that I would always do God's will, do it well and do it happily.

Then the words came to me, "Dear Mother, Queen of Peace, whom I believe is appearing to the children in Medugorje, please ask your Son to heal me anywhere I need to be healed. Your Son said that if you have faith and you say to a mountain, 'Move,' it will move. I believe, please help my unbelief."

As I asked Mary, Our Mother, to intercede for me, I felt a sudden surge of "electricity" run through me. I had experienced this feeling before, but it was always a very jolting and unpleasant experience. This time it was different. It felt soft, "bubbly" and very peaceful.

Throughout the next day many strange and wonderful things began to happen. When I returned home from La Roche College where I was taking a short course on the Gospels, I went to my downstairs bedroom to remove my leg braces. As I bent over to unfasten them I noticed my legs looked strange. I suddenly realized that they were straight! I was so overjoyed I cried out, yelling my tkanks to God and Mary. I took off my braces and using the crutches, went to the bottom of the flight of stairs which leads to the second floor.

I said to myself, "If I am cured, I can *run* up those stairs!"

I RAN up the stairs! Then I ran all over the place, laughing and crying with joy.

On Monday June 23, I was examined by my primary physician at Harmarville Rehabilitation Hospital in Pittsburgh, Pa. There was no trace of multiple sclerosis. All my reflexes were normal, my balance and muscle strength were normal, and the tremors were gone. The doctor couldn't believe it. He said in all his years he had never seen anything like this. All signs of deformity were gone, all spastic and severely atrophied muscles were completely restored in strength and function, and all paralysis was gone. He said I had been born again and had a second chance at life. "Go home, go to Church and thank God." These were his parting words. I am now in excellent health.

In 1987 I went to Medugorje, on the first anniversary of my healing, and prayed the Magnificat publicly in St. James Church to thank Jesus and Mary. I had been cured without even going to Medugorje and only went there to give thanks to the Queen of Peace and to Her Son, Jesus. ■

Rita Klaus
Pittsburgh, Pennsylvania

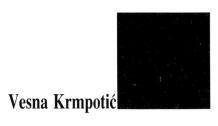

Vesna Krmpotić

A WELLSPRING AMID THE MOUNTAINS

'Tis in the water itself that we are brothers, not in the cup from which we drink

The poetry of Vesna Krmpotić, a famous contemporary croatian writer, is focused on a search for the mystic symbols of life, the presence of a divine unity in things; when touching on metaphysical themes her work shows the influence of oriental writers.

Places dissimilar make water different from water

There is a wellspring in Lebršnik, Herzegovina. So very cold, so icy is it that only eight pebbles may be plucked from its bed, and then the fingers become too numbed. In other parts, around Niš and Krapina, the springs are hot; water boils, it bubbles and it froths. And lest you scald your hand, no pebble may be taken from it either.

If it were for the hand to judge, it would deem the springs to be two different, even opposing, phenomena – the one that chills, the other that sears. But there is a judge above the hand; one who knows that differences are delusional and that the phenomena are but one – water. Indeed, when imagination and knowledge are allowed their rein, they will discern the drop which for that single moment burns as the drop that will, after endless journeys around the heavens and the earth, arrive at that icy fount beneath Lebršnik. That very drop!

'Tis in places unalike that water differs from water. It is ice and it is steam; it is neither hot nor cold; now a frantic eddy, now quiet, placid and at peace. It is in Tibet and on the Altiplano; beneath the Sahara and at the bottom of the oceans; on Madagascar and on Iceland; at Kamchatka and on the Marianas; on Sicily and Tasmania – but always it is that same water, the water of Lebršnik, water from my source – and it has been called all those names far removed, and reflected in it were faces of all colours; it has laved the bodies of every outline and has made them shine. It has comforted them, slaked their thirst and on returning to our spring carried no remembrance, but came as clean and as prepared for us as on the first dawning. In their passage around the earth, upon its crust, above it and beneath, all those drops have passed a million times through all the springs and along all the river beds.

Water: raining from above, issuing from below, and from wherever it wells, quenching thirst as it always does – damping the fires in man and beast and plant alike.

Vessels come in many hues but water it is neutral

We all delight in the cups from which we drink; few indeed are those who glorify te water. We all attempt to try our best for those cups, and that is as it should be. But should one declare the colour of his cup to be that of water, and should he further state that water is green, or, water is crimson, then he slights the water and he has but stirred antagonisms between our two cups.

These cups and founts, they are our cross – but not merely ours alone. How oft, how many times when that which belongs to all has been claimed as belonging to just one, to the exclusion of all; when that which in its very nature is intended to be all embracing, all reflecting, and when its universal boundlessness was confined. And how many times has a detail, a form, a modality, been embraced to be pronounced as the single, true manifestation of the essence. Obsessive adherence to one's own proclamations breeds intolerance, fear and, ultimately, hatred and violence – thereby betraying that essence we have all pledged to serve.

In truth, water does not take on the colour of the cup: the cup merely casts upon it the density of its nature. A screen does not adopt the image projected upon it – it only reflects it. Furthermore, water is not vessel-shaped; nor is it a chalice; nor is it cylindrical, nor droplet-like; it does not assume a priceless quality when thrust from alabaster fountains or jasper baths; neither is it denigrated by plate or clay. It is not made opalescent by moonlight, or blue from the heavens or by forests, green. It simply offers itself to our eyes to see it as we please and in the way to which we are accustomed. But as ever it has it assuages thirst in the same time honoured way.

Divine qualities

For there is something in that water, and in that earth, and in that air, and in that fire, and – aye – even in the very ether, which is above all mortal vision and comprehension: something we have not contributed and are therefore unable to lose; it is eternal, an infinitude. With water it is the fact that it both bathes and assuages; it overlays its maternal mantle across the unslaked needs of man and of his brethren – quadrupedal, winged and foliated alike; that it irrigates them and washes them, washes them and waters them, denying itself to none, asking no questions of who is whom or from where; infinitely unwavering in its insouciance of such considerations.

Those two facets of its properties – to soothe and to purify – are truly qualities divine; bestowals which solicit no returns since they are no more special than the very existence of the bestower.

Water may be drunk at all times of the year; it forms itself to every ewer and chagul and flows from every fountain. And therein lies its intangible, mysterious, miraculous and wondrous essence. The suffering she must have undergone, this mother water – she, whose desire so burns to quell the flames; how much she must have grieved when furious turmoils erupted beside her springs, and in her very name.

Imperishable residuums

And yes, wars have been fought over the colour and the shape of a cup. Our vessel was extolled and our aqueducts exalted, and he who chose not to drink from it was deemed to be unworthy of the water, and yes, even of drinking. The flames of war blazed mindless and insatiable, and the leaden ashes of the innocent were strewn across the lands. And still today they fall continuously from the upper layers of the air, those immortal substances – the ashes, the *vibhuti,* the imperishable nucleus remains that is a symbol of immortality. The solitary matter that will not relume when introduced to fire.

Would that winds of wisdom and fresh thought and deeper insight blow, and scatter those ashes to all points; for all corners of the earth must be infused with remembrance of what is mortal and, through that infusion, that which is immortal in its mortality.

Magna Mater in five movements

It is not just water that is mother. So too is earth.

The most enduring resonance of sound, at the limit of five elements. Earth corresponds to the body, the fundamental pia mater of a being. Earth sustains – bread, fruit and honey come therefrom; the voice of the earth is the sound of a drum, the stamping of feet. Feet become weary from treading on it, but the earth never becomes tired of being walked upon.

Some mother too is fire. A wild, red-haired cresset curvetting from the air; warming, searing, illuminating. And around it – air, resident in every breast, a universal breath. Still more delicate than air is ether, *akash,* the all-pervading cosmic primordial matter that imbues all, with which all is imbued, imprinted into which is every form, every name, every thought, every event. It is through those five facets, from their interplay and permutations, that the world is made so colourful.

From the compact earth to insubstantial ether, from the sublime ether towards humble earth, along the terraces of air, fire and water to the sounds of bells, gongs and harps, the mysterious, magnificent and wondrous Magna Mater – the energy of loving– manifests herself to us.

The fin of the fish and the wing of the bird

Nine years ago, in a corner of the world which on this occasion chanced to be here, in Yugoslavia, in Herzegovina, in a region otherwise unknown but for the ravages of wartime and of the post-war era, sprang forth such a potent wellspring of maternal water of life: an event that humbles intellect or endeavours to be superior to, but which can never equal reason. The form taken by this issuing was the Mother of God, Our Catholic Lady. For a full nine years now, the apparition of Our Lady has appeared to the eyes of a small number of young people every day, at the same hour. Those visions have set in motion a chain of transphysical and other supernatural events that have, for just as many years, been the subject of investigation, research and explanation both by individuals and commissions and which are causing profound emotional reactions and quiet tremors.

All of this has evolved within a sacral triangle delineated by three points – the Mount of Križevac, the Mount of Apparitions and the parish church. Here, learning may be likened to some ancient and decorative dagger, while fantasy and language are but adumbration.

Those who ascribe a meaning to the matters of spirit and soul through a body, and who view them from the aspect of a body, see in the phenomenon a conscious move on the part of the locals who are eager to make capital from it. (And there is no doubt that handsome profits are to be made by both locals and visitors alike – as has ever been the case where people gather in great numbers). Others, like minded, add their own views to the foregoing judgment: that it is a masquerade concocted through the politics of Catholicism, combined with the hormonal disturbances of the young.

If a certain phenomenon is found by an investigator to be inexplicable, beyond his sensibilities to explain or outside his experience and the perceptive powers of his mind and reasoning, then how can his judgment on such a phenomenon have any serious merit? If the greater element of the discussion regarding the supernatural be absent from apperception, as it must be, how then is one able to judge the supernatural from the aspect of the material and its pertaining reasons, viewpoints and criteria? It would be just as if a fish were to attempt to understand the existence of a bird, arriving at the conclusion that it must be an imposter since, as fish have known since time out of memory, there can be no life outside water and that there is no other way of making progress except with fins.

Peace that is no interlude between two wars

But nothing is served by wrangling about it – about what is and of what kind is the phenomenon of Our Lady of Međugorje. Let us leave the explanations to the interpreters of the future – we shall not be kept waiting overlong. For us now the most important thing is to learn the source the inspires the phenomenon, its effect, consequence and path. Let us be, for a moment, pragmatic. We are able to grasp Our Lady by the trail she leaves. Electrons are also identified by the trace they leave – and so what, who, gives thought to not having seen the foot?

The word that echoes most frequently through the Triangle that is Međugorje is PEACE. People who happen to travel to this Triangle, be it as pilgrims, informants of officialdom or as interested but unofficial onlookers, are either overwhelmed by that word and that atmosphere, or it gusts through them, or it pervades them. In 1988 two million people wended their undulatory way through Međugorje. These are indeed united nations, unaccredited but spontaneous but effectively in the name of the same goal as the United Nations Organization: Peace; international and planetary. No more urgent task obtains in this heliocentric system.

Peace, in the sense of Međugorje, is not an interlude between two wars but a peace that is a lasting state, come what may – action good or bad or contemplation, within us or without. It is profoundly individual as a realization, and supremely supraindividual as an aim and as an influence. Such PEACE is not a state of passivity or indifference, as many would think. Quite the opposite. In a state of PEACE long banked, wellsprings are reopened and a tide of energy both spiritual and physical begins to course through one. To be confronted within oneself by that river and its radiation is to experience what the religious term purification and illumination. This process possesses its own rhythm and proceeds at its own pace in everyone but in places where massive energy focuses, acceleration of tremendous scale occurs. That being the pertinence of phenomenal places, permeable sites, white holes and synapses through which a message percolates into our universe from a superior dominion.

People who are irradiated by PEACE for even a short spell begin to transmit it to others; they begin to glow as if a victim of radium. They are fundamentally different from the people they were before the experience: the code of their being is altered and the order of their values changed.

Every such Triangle leaves the world a little different: it becomes a little lighter every time. No statistics are to be found on this – there is just tradition, which does not care for publicity – at least for now.

Conditions for unconditionality

The great Hindu Islamic guru, Nanak, once entered a mosque in Kashmir and prostrated himself towards the north, or it may have been to the south, or possibly the east. A sheikh advised him that Allah was west of him, in the direction of Mecca. "Show me a direction, in which He is not", said Nanak, also bowing towards the west.

This was necessary to enlighten the narrow-minded sheikh. That does not however mean that specific rituals of individual faith and sanctuaries should not be respected – provided of course that beside being in Mecca, Allah is everywhere; and it is that feeling which matters during prostrations, not regulation. Or else we shall again not discern the infinitely various colour of water from the colour of glass.

Water belongs to all. Certain glasses belong to certain people, periods, cultures, civilizations. But whatever our glass may be that we have brought to lift the water, it is the drinking of it that matters. The well of Međugorje belongs to all. The sole condition is that no drinker imposes his or her tumbler upon others. Only thus are the drinkers in harmony with earth, water, fire, air and, aye, with ether, which know no limitations or conditions to the giving.

The mother people

Glowing within me is a live ember of yearning to speak through Međugorje about the matters troubling my Croatian people as well as those people with whom I live, the Serbs: these are the two peoples to whom I owe as much grattitude, respect and understanding as I am capable of having and of giving.

Sathya Sai Baba says that your people, your country, your culture and your faith are your mother. She has given you birth and nurtured you and for that you respect her as you do the creative principle in a human form. Your mother may be profligate and an inebriate, lame and ignorant, just as she may be a lady possessed of outstanding charm, a righteous darling of plenitude – but all those characteristis should have no bearing on your love and gratitude (says Sai Baba).

For man does not love his own because it is the best and most advantageous, rather because it has been given to him to love and has been entrusted to him as a task and a duty of self-denial. Love for one's mother, one's homeland, culture and faith should succour and not be a barrier to accepting the love that others bear for their mother, their nation, homeland and faith. A condition for true mutuality is the correct approach of non-exclusivistic love for one's self and for one's own. For how is one able to love and exalt one's mother whilst at the same time harbouring nothing but disdain for the mother of another? Recognizing that somewhere in the depths of the species and the collective soul our roots are common, where is the sense in imprecating evil on the neighbouring bough?

A monodrama people

In this country drinking was, and is still, done from disparate cups: now one would top up another's, then a second, now a third, Regrettably, the experience of respect for divergencies which comes naturally from human magnanimity and not from some political, unspontaneous and selfish motives, is not in our genes. Much less the experience of recognizing the common in the unlike.

We are a monodrama people; our greatest talent lies in self-opinionatedness. We, different Yugoslavs, do not distinguish the same water in different cups; we are atavistically unsympathetic towards dissimilarities. Our subconscious is a reticulation of guilt and bitterness, rage and remorse; it is a free arena of Furies and Erinyes – and this pain has never been plumbed by shallow political probes. Politics concerns itself with the human skin, not the soul.

What the wise ones say

However, the soul will, as the wise ones tell us, cast out everything that is foreign – both politics and history. Everything that is fateful turmoils both people and things. It first occurs in the cave of one's heart, behind the wall that is the forehead; in the cellars of the thalamus and in the attics of the epiphysis; in the vestiges of those ancestors who have not yet submitted. Subsequently, man sifts through the consequences of all those inner schemings, placing the responsibility on those fantastic circumstances (and what would we do without them), devoting his feverish energy to "resolving" the same.

This what is and that which is not are the true consequences of we ourselves. Becoming ready at the same moment is the cause of what shall be and what shall not. It is time (and how long it has been so) for us to commence coping with causes, to begin influencing our own destiny.

So that which was unimportant becomes important; so that ethical education becomes more important than the academic

Coping with causes. Does this not mean to concern oneself with ameliorating the spirit and the soul on a different and long-term basis? That is to say, the cultivation of virtues and character? Forbearance and self-denial, compassion, courage, sincerity, a pious attitude towards all life – by whom and where is all that taught except in religious schools? Our "educational" institutions offer no such teaching. And yet such education is the only politics that has any hope of success, even during tragic confrontations on a massive scale between peoples, tribes, families and individuals. The creation and moulding of a more favourable *karma* of a people begins with ethical education, starting at a very early age. It is time for ethical education to be given a greater priority than the academic.

The time has generally come for that which was important to become unimportant – and which intends to remain so. It is time that the symbol lost its significance, but that its sum and substance be carried with love. The national emotions of Croats, Serbs, Albanians and others are signs; their meaning is devotion to country and the wholesomeness of its traditions which does not exclude – but rather includes – others, recognizing itself within them.

It is time not only that it became irrelevant who is a Serb, a Slovene or a Macedonian, but also who is a Yugoslav, a Tungus or an Arab. It is time not only for national chauvinism to pass away, but also for that of the state; not merely individual, municipal, tribal and republican chauvinism, but also geopolitical, racial, churchly and religious, as well as that of blocs. Either all people are brothers or nobody is anyone's brother. If he fails to give paramountcy to the "caste of man" rather than to blood, geography and history, to cultural-physical environments, mankind will create enclaved brotherhoods – brotherhoods by cup, and not by water.

Necessity and not merit

All is clear in word but come the deed black atavisms appear and intellect becomes the ancilla of instinct – and instinct dictates that reasons be found for departure from the laws of unselfishness.

Are we worthy people simply by being good Croats, Serbs or Tungus, good Orthodox, Catholics or Muslims; or are we worthy Albanians, Armenians and others because we are primarily good and worthy people? It is absurd even to pose the question – we all quite clearly know the answer even while the words hang. But come the deeds responses soon metamorphose and evidence a quite inverted order of priority.

Let the depths of my humanity be as much a passe-partout for my Croatianism as for any other second or third cachet. And from those depths I wish to say to the Serbian people, with whom for so many years I have shared a beautiful life, that we have been presented with an excellent opportunity for sobering down, and then to make our peace before the mountain trail of the message that emanates from Međugorje. My Serbian friends ask me: Why just here, and not somewhere else? Who is able to fully answer such a question? Why in Palestine, and not somewhere else? Some things must remain veiled from us – at least for the time being. But in any event, Međugorje is not "ours" and it is not "theirs" – it belongs to the whole world since its address is to the world, and the world comes to it. The next well-intentioned question: How is it that Our Lady chose to appear here around the anniversary of when a number of Serbs were killed in a nearby village? That very date and the close proximity of that pit ... it must surely be, it is believed, some Catholic-Ustashi deviousness revealing itself. But what if Our Lady appeared here *for just that very reason*, here where the wraiths of history are so sanguineous and still unsated? And where June 24 was fateful for the Serbs of that region? I am able to offer no other answer except in the form of an analogy: in an area plagued by malaria there grows a cinchona tree. A mother's energy is devoted to those of her children who have fallen prey to sickness and to disharmony. It is a matter of necessity, not merit.

Spirit is a home to spirit

It is time to give no thought to which is "our" terrain and which is "theirs", when concerning oneself with spirit and spirituality. Christianity today is not most widespread in the land that gave Christ birth; on the contrary, it attracts a greater following in the countries He never visited, countries where bitter battles were waged against Christianity. Nor was Buddha born where today Buddhism is omnipresent. Matters of spirit do not recognize territorial appropriations, since spirit can find no other home but spirit.

And so it is that the wellspring of Međugorje je is offered to all, and no energy or perspective should be lost on the question of from "whose" territory the has water sprung (on this occasion).

Mother of people and mother of man

Our Lady is, in her own words, mother to all people. Regardless of whether or not one believes in such things as the Universal mother it is possible to understand it, to a degree, through one's own mother.

Each man has just the one mother. This is the most wondrous, most beautiful and divine fact of motherhood: all else can be multiple – brothers and sisters, wives and children, friends and acquaintances – but a mother is one and not selected; you cannot replace her with another, you can deny her but never alter the fact that she gave you life. In this there is no difference between a beggar and a king, and in that respect, I dare say, all people are of the same mind.

A mother is man's first mentor, his first homeland, first nourishment, his first protective embrace. She is also a symbol of the country that reared him, the faith that developed him, the language that made him a civilized being and the traditions that honed his senses for permanence of certain values. He therefore owes her a debt of respect and gratitude. I have deliberately omitted mention of love – for this is something that cannot be owed, being in its essence a causeless category, not to be exchanged for beneficence and outside the range of reciprocal moves.

And being mindful of the fact that there are around two billion mothers breathing and loving at this moment on planet Earth, and that within each one of them resides, to a greater or lesser degree, the instinct for protecting and nourishing her offspring, then the concept that the state of motherhood is the tie that binds and the thread that courses through all those individual pearls of flesh and blood is not so far removed. Participating in this universal citizenship is a characteristic of everyone ever born. Pan-motherhood, the filament of that string of pearls appears in man's mythologies and religions as the *avatar* of a principle and a condition. Mothers of man are delegates of that condition and principle, his delegates of tangible matter.

Through his own "delegate" man also makes contact with this untouchable Magna Mater, a transcendental principle which occasionally descends into human history also, but which is attired in robes characteristic of both the time and the place in which it appears. The statement „I am the mother of all people" in this perspective appears not only as a calling card of a Being (who walked this Earth 2000 years ago), but also as a Universal Id, multiplied in all the mothers of the world.

Peace and reconciliation

A name and a form are essential to the category of a cup. Maria, Isis, Tara, Parvati – and, does anybody know, what was her name in Atlantis and in Lemuria? All those names that people have given her, all those different names ... What matters is that she did and does answer to them all.

Our land is in turmoil and it is not to be pacified by the nostrums to be found in a politician's pharmacy. I am personally convinced that it can be calmed only by other, diferent means – through recognition that we are brothers, not just Yugoslav, Slavic and of the Earth, but brothers by the same supranational and supraterrestial principle.

Let us return to the question of what it is that is happenning in Međugorje, and why just there?

Let us assume that mother's children are at daggers drawn – as indeed they are; let us assume that they have wronged each other – as they have; let us assume that they have not asked each other's forgiveness – as they have not; let us assume that they are devising beds of nails one for the other – as they are. What will the mothers do and where will they go? A flesh and blood mother, mother of our body, a delegate of Pan-motherhood – what will she do and how will she fare? Will she not stand at the boundaries drawn between the houses and fields of her children, to call on them to assemble, and to calm them down? Will she not venture to where the fires are most fierce, and pain most intense? And where earthquakes are imminent, should not the tremors of the soul be soothed?

Unsoothed herself, how is she able to sooth her charges? Hence the emphasis on PEACE as a condition of any reconciliation. This PEACE emanates from a source within Everyman and which has for so long been banked. The *Avtars* tell us that this is their task – to tap this inner source.

Why should we join issue as to whether Our Lady of Međugorje is an hallucination or a reality at higher frequencies? Why should we not understand her as an opportunity to reach one another through that which every man holds sacred and dear, through a mother? ■

Mauro Harsch

A LETTER FROM BOMBAY

I find myself in Valiv, a small village 70 km from Bombay which abounds with tropical vegetation, palms and flowers – a veritable oasis of peace and untainted air.

Surrounded by a crowd of delighted children with traditional haircuts, I have just performed the ceremonial opening of Villa Angels (this is what they have called our house), a beautiful and solid, pink building that had been modified into a number of different sections that it can accept one hundred orphans up the age of 18.

Following the blessing of the premises and a presentation of gifts to the children in honour of the foundation, I was literally »attacked« by the children. Never before in my life have I met so many sensitive, well brought up, warm-hearted and intelligent children. With touching spontaneity they showed me each detail of the house and garden, the crib and the statue of the Madonna...

It is surprising to what extent my experience of a week in Bombay recalls the feelings that filled me during my conversion in Međugorje. That same desperation that engulfed me on the first day in that hamlet in Yugoslavia I felt once again yesterday in Bombay when passing through the slums, in which hundreds of thousands of people live in indescribable conditions. The joy that I felt in the church in Međugorje I again experienced among the children of Valiv.

The was a sign that I have received many times and which has anchored me deeply in the Cristian faith in Providence and in the Church. In the Church, the aim of which is to strongly preserve the faith that manifests itself in love towards others, and which eschews any act that results in divisions and misunderstandings that could be harmful to Christian unity.

I shall remember always the genuine warmth of the children of Valiv, which brought back a feeling of pure joy that I have not experienced since childhood.

Only those who have not had a similar experience can believe that aid for the Third World is unnecessary, describing it as a drop in the ocean. Many children who would have been doomed to an early death from starvation or to prostitution have been saved. Two hundred of them are by my side.

They are happy children whose needs are small and with only one great desire – to LEARN, so that one day they would be able to work and assist other children to escape from the terrible situation that oppresses them. Many children are waiting for OUR help right now, today; and without it they will not be able to survive. In Bombay I have realized that their lives depend upon us. Our small, personal sacrifices can save millions of children.

Miracles can happen through our faith.

While writing these lines, I remain convinced that many artists and other people of good will are going to help with the aims and ideas born in Međugorje.

Tonight, deliberating on the day just past, it seems to me that I have just awakened from a beautiful dream – but I have not; what happened in Valiv today was reality...!   (1.1.1990) ■

MESSAGES OF OUR LADY
TO THE PARISH OF MEĐUGORJE

March 1, 1984   **Special choice of the parish**

Dear children! I have chosen this parish in a special way and I wish to lead it. I am guarding it in love and I want everyone to be mine. Thank you for having responded tonight. I wish you always to be with me and my Son in ever greater numbers. I shall speak a message to you every Thursday.

March 8, 1984   **All are called to conversion**

Thank you for having responded to my call! Dear children, you in the parish, be converted. This is my other wish. That way all those who shall come here shall be able to convert.

March 15, 1984   **Perpetual Adoration of the Blessed Sacrament**

Tonight also, dear children, I am grateful to you in a special way for beiong here. Unceasingly adore the Most Blessed Sacrament of the Altar. I am always present when the faithful are adoring. Special graces are then being received.

March 22, 1984   **Honoring the wounds of Jesus**

Dear children! In a special way this evening I am calling you during Lent to honor the wounds of my Son, which He received from the sins of this parish. Unite yourselves with my prayers for the parish so that His sufferings may be bearable. Thank you for having responded to my call. Try to come in ever greater numbers.

March 29, 1984   **Perseverance in trials**

Dear children! In a special way this evening I am calling you to perseverance in trials. Consider how the Almighty is still suffering today on account of your sins. So when sufferings come, offer them up as a sacrifice to God. Thank you for having responded to my call.

April 5, 1984   **Reparation to the Sacred Heart of Jesus**

Dear children! This evening I pray you especially to venerate the Heart of my Son, Jesus. Make reparation for the wound inflicted on the Heart of my Son. That Heart is offended by all kinds of sin. Thank you for coming this evening.

April 12, 1984   **Pray for unity in the parish**

Dear children! Today I beseech you to stop slandering and to pray for the unity of the parish, because I and my Son have a special plan for this parish. Thank you for having responded to my call.

April 19, 1984 (Holy Thursday)   **Pray with me!**

Dear children! Sympathize with me! Pray, pray, pray!

April 26, 1984   **No message was given by Our Lady**

April 30, 1984 (Monday)   **I do not wish to force anyone**

Marija asked Our Lady, Dear Madonna, why didn't you give me a message for the parish on Thursday? Our Lady replied, I don't wish to force anyone to do that which he/she neither feels nor desires, even though I had special messages for the parish by which I wanted to awaken the faith of every believer. But only a really small number has accepted my Thursday messages. In the beginning there were quite a few. But it's become a routine affait for them. And now recently some are asking for the message out of curiosity, and not out of faith and devotion to my Son and me.

May 3, 1984   **No message was given by Our Lady**

May 10, 1984   **Our Lady will go on giving messages**

Many of the faithful felt shaken by the last message of Our Lady. Some had the feeling that Our Lady would not give any more messages to the parish, but this evening she said, I am speaking to you and I wish to speak further. You, just listen to my instructions!

May 17, 1984   **Consecration to Mary wins special graces**

Dear chilren! Today I am very happy because there are many who want to consecrate themselves to me. Thank you. You have not made a mistake. My Son, Jesus Christ, wishess to bestow on you special graces through me. My Son is happy because of your dedication. Thank you for having responded to my call.

May 24, 1984   **A Mother's love for all**

Dear chilren! I have told you already that I have chosen you in a special way, just the way you are. I, the Mother, love you all. And in any moment that is difficult for you, do not be afraid! Because I love you even then when you are far from me and my Son. Please, do not let my heart weep with tears of blood because of the souls who are lost in sin. Therefore, dear children, pray, pray, pray! Thank you for having responded to my call.

May 31, 1984 (Ascension Thursday)   **Message to be given Saturday**

There were many people present from abroad. Our Lady did not give a message for the parish. The told Marija that she would give a message on Saturday to be announced at the Sunday parish Mass.

June 2, 1984 (Saturday)   **Novena to the Holy Spirit**

Dear children! Tonight I wish to tell you during the days of this novena to pray for the outpouring of the Holy Spirit on your families and on your parish. Pray, and you shall not regret it. God will give you gifts by which you will glorify Him till the end of your life on this earth. Thank you for having responded to my call.

June 9, 1984 (Saturday)   **Pray for the Spirit of Truth**

Dear children! Tomorrow night pray for the Spirit of Truth! Especially, you from the parish. Because you need the Spirit of Truth to be able to convey the messages just the way they are, neither adding anything to them, nor taking anything whatsoever away from them, but just the way I said them. Pray for the Holy Spirit to ionspire you with the spirit of prayer, so you will pray more. I, your Mother, tell you that you are praying little. Thank you for having responded to my call.

June 14, 1984   **No message was given by Our Lady**

June 21, 1984   **Keep on praying**

Pray, pray, pray! Thank you for having responded to my call.

June 28, 1984   **No message was given by Our Lady**

July 12, 1984   **Sharing victory over Satan with Jesus**

Dear children! These days Satan wants to frustrate my plans. Pray that his plan not be realized. I will pray my to Son Jesus to give you the grace to experience the victory of Jesus in the temptations of Satan. Thank you for having responded to my call.

July 19, 1984   **I am with you during temptations**

Dear children! These days you have been experiencing how Satan is working. I am always with you, and don't you be afraid of temptations because God is always watching over us. Also I have given myself to you and I sympathize with you even in the smallest temptation. Thank you for having responded to my call.

July 26, 1984   **Persistence in prayer and penance**

Dear children! Today also I wish to call you to persistent prayer and penance. Especially, let the young people of this parish be more active in their prayers. Thank you for having responded to my call.

August 2, 1984   **More prayer for conversion of sinners**

Dear children! Today I am joyful and I thank you for your prayers. Pray still more these days for the conversion of sinners. Thank you for having responded to my call.

August 9, 1984   **No message was given by Our Lady**

August 11, 1984 (Saturday)   **Prayer and surrender to Jesus**

Dear children! Pray, because Satan wishes to complicate my plans still further. Pray with the heart and surrender yourselves to Jesus in prayer.

August 14, 1984 (Tuesday)   **Strict fast and the full rosary**

This apparition was unexpected. Ivan was prayings at home. After that he started to get ready to go to Church for the evening services. By surprise Our Lady appeared to him and told him to relate to the people. *I would like the people to pray along with me these days. And to pray as much as possible! And to fast strictly on Wednesdays and Fridays, and every day to pray at least one Rosary: the joyful, sorrowful and glorious mysteries.* Our Lady asked that we accept this message with a firm will. She especially requested this of the parishioners and the faithful of the surrounding places.

August 16, 1984   **Live and spread my messages**

Dear children! I beseech you, especially those from this parish, to live my messages and convey them to others, to whomever you meet. Thank you for haviong responded to my call.

August 23, 1984   **Always more prayer**

Dear children! Pray, pray! Marija said that she also invited the people, and especially the young people, to keep order during the Mass.

August 30, 1984   **Pray on the Cross Mountain**

Dear children! The cross was also in God's plan when you built it. These days, especially, go on the mountain and pray before the cross. I need your prayers. Thank you for having responded to my call.

September 6, 1984   **Pray at the cross for peace**

Dear children! Without prayer there is no peace. Therefore I say to you, dear children, pray at the foot of the cross for peace. Thank you for having responded to my call.

September 13, 1984   **Pray that Jesus conquers**

Dear children! I still need your prayers. You wonder why all these prayers? Look around you, dear children, and you will see how greatly sin has dominated the world. Pray, therefore, that Jesus conquers. Thank you for having responded to my call.

September 20, 1984   **Fasting and prasying with the heart**

Dear children! Today I call on you top begin fasting with the heart. There are many people who are fasting, but only because everyone is fasting. It has become a custom which no one wants to stop. I ask the parish to fast out of gratitude because God has allowed me to stay this long in this parish. Dear children, fast and pray with the heart. Thank you for having responded to my call.

September 27, 1984   **Praying the family rosary**

Dear children! You have helped me along by your prayers to realize my plans. Keep on praying that my plans be completely realized. I request the families of the parish to pray the family rosary. Thank you for having responded to my call.

October 4, 1984   **Your prayers make my happy**

Dear children! Today I want to tell you that again and again you make me happy by your prayer, but there are enough of those in this very parish who do not pray and my heart is saddened. Therefore pray that I can bring all your sacrifices and prayers to the Lord. Thank you for haviong responded to my call.

October 8, 1984 (Monday)   **Evening family rosary for sinners**

(Jakov was sick and received this message at home.) Dear children, Let all the prayers you say in your homes in the evening be for the conversion of sinners because the world is in great sin. Every evening pray the rosary.

October 11, 1984   **God tests those whom he loves**

Dear children! Thank you for dedicating all your hard work to God even now when He is testing you through the grapes you are picking. Be assured, dear children, that He loves you and, therefore, He tests you. You just always offer up all your burdens to God and do not be anxious. Thank you for having responded to my call.

October 18, 1984   **Home Bible reading daily**

Dear children! Today I call on you to read the Bible every day in your homes and let it be in a visible place so as always to encourage you to read it and to pray. Thank you for having responded to my call.

October 25, 1984   **Special October graces**

Dear children! Pray during this month. God allows me every day to help you with graces to defend yourselves against evil. This is my month. I want to give it to you. You just pray and God will give you the graces you are seeking. I will help along with it. Thank you for having responded to my call.

November 1, 1984   **First place for prayer in the family**

Dear children! Today I call you to the renewal of prayer in your homes. The work in the fields is over. Now devote yourselves to prayer. Let prayer take the first place in your families. Thank you for having responded to my call.

November 8, 1984   **Praying to grasp these great graces**

Dear children! You are not conscious of the messages which God is sending you through me. He is giving you great graces and you do not comprehend them. Pray to the Holy Spirit for enlightenment. If you only knew how great are the graces God is granting you, you would be praying without ceasing. Thank you for having responded to my call.

November 15, 1984   **Comprehending God's love and mine**

Dear children! You are a chosen people and God has given you great graces. You are not conscious of every message which I am giving you. Now I just want to say – pray, pray, pray! I don't know what else to tell you because I love you and I want you to comprehend my love and God's love through prayer. Thank you for having responded to my call.

November 22, 1984   **Root the messages in your hearts**

Dear children! These days live all the main messages and keep rooting them in your hearts till Thursday. Thank you for having responded to my call.

November 29, 1984   **Listening and praying out of love**

Dear children! No, you don'ts know how to love and you don't know how to listen with love to the words I am saying to you. Be conscious, my beloved, that I am yout Mother and I have come on earth to teach you to listen out of love, to pray out of love and not compelled by the fact that you are carrying a cross. By means of the cross God is glorified through every person. Thank you for having responded to my call.

December 6, 1984   **Accepting my messages for Christmas**

Dear children! These days I am calling you to family prayer. In God's Name many times I have been giving you messages, but you have not listened to me. This Christmas will be unforgettable for you only if you accept the messages which I am giving you. Dear children, don't allow that day of joy to become my most sorrowful day. Thank you for having responded to my call.

Zlata Vucelić

CELEBRATING THE CROSS

■ After walking 40 kilometers to Međugorje

December 13, 1984   **A week for learning to love**

D*ear children! You know that the season of joy is getting closer, but without love you will achieve nothing. So first of all, begin to love your own family, everyone in the parish, and then you'll be able to love and accept all who are coming over here. Now let these seven days be a week when you need to learn to love. Thank you for having responded to my call.*

December 20, 1984   **Flowers for Jesus**

D*ear children! Today I am inviting you to do something concrete for Jesus Christ. As a sign of dedication to Jesus I want each family of the parish to bring a single flower before that happy day. I want every member of the family to have a single flower by the crib so Jesus can come and see your dedication to Him! Thank you for having responded to my call.*

December 21, 1984   **Like flowers blooming for Jesus**

I *want you to be a flower which will blossom for Jesus on Christmas. And a flower that will not stop blooming when Christmas is over. I want your hearts to be shepherds to Jesus* [Message given through Jelena Vasilj].

December 27, 1984   **Happy hearts defeated Satan**

D*ear children! This Christmas Satan wanted in a special way to spoil God's plans. You, dear children, have discerned Satan even on Christmas day itself. But God is winning in all your hearts. So let your hearts keep on being happy. Thank you for having responded to my call.*

January 3, 1985   **A week of thanksgiving for graces**

D*ear children! These days the Lord has bestowed upon you great graces. Let this week be one of thanksgiving for all the graces which God has granted you. Thank you for having responded to my call.*

January 10, 1985   **The faithful ones keep me coming**

D*ear children! Today I want to thank you for all your sacrifices, but special thanks to those who have become dear to my heart and come here gladly. There are enough parishoners who are not listening to the messages, but because of those who are in a special way close to my heart, because of them I am giving them because I love you and I want you to spread my messages with your heart. Thank you for having responded to my call.*

January 14, 1985 (Monday)   **Withstanding Satan by constant prayer**

M*y dear children! Satan is so strong and with all his might wants to disturb my plans which I have begun with you. You pray, just pray and don't stop for a minute! I will pray to my Son for the realization of all the plans I have begun. Be patient and constant in your prayers. And don't let Satan discourage you. He is working hard in the world. Be on your guard!* [Message conveyed by Vicka From Our Lady]

January 17, 1985 (Monday)   **Withstanding Satan by mass and prayer**

D*ear children! These days Satan is working underhandedly against this parish, and you, dear children, have fallen asleep in prayer, and only some are going to Mass. Withstand the days of temptation! Thank you for having responded to my call.*

January 24, 1985   **Renewal and prayer assure happines**

D*ear children! These days you have experienced God's sweetness through the renewals which have been in this parish. Satan wants to work still more fiercely to take away your joy from each one of you. By prayer you can completely disarm him and ensure your happiness. Thank you for having responded to my call.*

January 31, 1985   **Hearts open like flowers to the sun**

D*ear children! Today I wish to tell you to open your hearts to God like the spring flowers which crave for the sun. I am your Mother and I always want you to be closer to the Father and that He will always give abundant gifts to your hearts. Thank you for having responded to my call.*

February 7, 1985   **God is glorified in Satan's defeat**

D*ear children! These days Satan is manifesting himself in a special way in this parish. Pray, dear children, that God's plan is brought into effect and that every work of Satan ends up for the glory of God. I have stayed with you this long so I might help you along in your trials. Thank you for having responded to my call.*

February 14, 1985   **Listen to me and live my messages**

D*ear children! Today is the day when I give you a message for the parish, but the whole parish is not accepting the messages and it not living them. I am saddened and I want you, dear children, to listen to me and to live my messages. Every family must pray family prayer and read the Bible! Thank you for having responded to my call.*

February 21, 1985   **For Lent start living my message out of love**

D*ear children! From day to day I have been inviting you to renewal and prayer in the parish, but you are not accepting it. Today I am calling you for the last time! Now it's Lent and you as a parish can turn to my message during Lent out of love. If you don't do that, I don't wish to keep on giving messages. God is permitting me that. Thank you for having responded to my call.*

February 28, 1985   **Living in God's love**

D*ear children! Today I call you to live the word this week: »I love God!« Dear children through love you will achieve everything and even what you think is impossible. God wants this parish to belong completely to Him. And thats what I want too. Thank you for having responded to my call.*

March 7, 1985   **Renewal of family prayer**

Dear children! Today I call you to renew prayer in your families. Dear children, encourage the very young prayer and the children to go to Holy Mass. Thank you for having responded to my call.

March 14, 1985   **Giving light to those in darkness**

Dear children! In your life you have all experienced light and darkness. God grants to every person to recognize good and evil. I am calling you to the light which you should carry to all the people who are in darkness. People who are in darkness daily come into your homes. Dear children, give them the light! Thank you for having responded to my call.

March 21, 1985   **Urgent call to accept Our Lady**

Dear children! I wish to keep on giving messages and therefore today I call you to live and accept my messages! Dear children, I love you and in a special way I have chosen this parish, one more dear to me than the others, in which I have gladly remained when the Almighty sent me. Therefore I call on you – accept me, dear children, that it might go well with you. Listen to my messages! Thank you for having responded to my call.

March 24, 1985 (Sunday)   **Confession and Reconciliation**

Today I wish to call you all to confession, even if you have confessed a few days ago. I wish that you all experience my feast day within yourselves. But you cannot experience it unless you abandon yourselves completely to God. Therefore, I am inviting you all to reconciliation with God!

March 28, 1985   **Urgency of prayer**

Dear children! Today I wish to call you to pray, pray, pray! In prayer you shall perceive the greatest joy and the way out of every situation that has no exit. Thak you for starting up prayer. Each individual is dear to my heart. And I thank all who have urged prayer in their families. Thank you for having responded to my call.

April 4, 1985 (Holy Thursday)   **My messages will continue**

Dear children! I thank you for having started to think more about God's glory in your hearts. Today is the day when I wished to stop giving the messages because some individuals did not accept me. The parish has been moved and I wish to keep on giving you messages as it has never been in history from the beginning of the world. Thank you for having responded to my cal.

April 5, 1985 (Good Friday)   **Carry the cross with Christ**

You parishioners have a great and heavy cross, but don't be afraid to carry it. My Son is here who will help you. [message given through Ivanka]

April 11, 1985   **Need for special light of the Holy Spirit**

Dear children! Today I wish to say to everyone in the parish to pray in a special way to the Holy Spirit for enlightenment. From today God wishes to test the parish in a special way in order that He might strengthen it in faith. Thank you for having responded to my call.

April 18, 1985   **Happiness for open hearts**

Dear children! Today I thank you for every opening of your hearts. Joy overtakes me for every heart that is opened to God especially from the parish. Rejoice with me! Pray all the prayers for the opening of sinful hearts. I desire that. God desires that through me. Thank you for having responded to my call.

April 25, 1985   **Cultivate the heart for a new spirit**

Dear children! Today I wish to tell you to begin to work in your hearts as you are working in the fields. Work and change your hearts so that a new spirit from God can take its place in your hearts. Thank you for having responded to my call.

May 2, 1985   **Pray with the heart always**

Dear children! Today I call you to prayer with the heart, and not just from habit. Some are coming but do not wish to move ahead in prayer. Therefore, I wish to warn you like a Mother: pray that prayer prevails in your hearts in every moment. Thank you for having responded to my call.

May 9, 1985   **Seek things of heaven rather than of earth**

Dear children! No, you do not know how many graces God is giving you. You do not want to move ahead during these days when the Holy Spirit is working in a special way. Your hearts are turned toward the things of earth and they preoccupy you. Turn your hearts toward prayer and seek the Holy Spirit to be poured out on you. Thank you for having responded to my call.

May 16, 1985   **Mass: experience of God**

Dear children! I am calling you to a more active prayer and attendance at Holy Mass. I wish your Mass to be an experience of God. I wish especially to say to the young people: be open to the Holy Spirit because God wishes to draw you to Himself in these days when Satan is at work. Thank you for having responded to my call.

May 16, 1985   **Surrender to Jesus and the Spirit**

Dear children! These days I call you especially to open your hearts to the Holy Spirit. Especially during these days the Holy Spirit is working through you. Open your hearts and surrender your life to Jesus so that He works through your hearts and strengthens you in faith. Thank you for having responded to my call.

May 30, 1985   **Prayer is your joy and rest**

Dear children! I call you again to prayer with the heart. Let prayer, dear children, be your every day food in a special way when your work in the fields is so wearing you out that you cannot pray with the heart. Pray, and then you shall overcome even every weariness. Prayer will be your joy and your rest. Thank you for having responded to my call.

■ The Way of the Cross on Mt. Križevac

June 6, 1985   **Loving family and pilgrims**

Dear children! During these days people from all nations will be coming into the parish. And now I am calling you to love: love first of all your own household members, and then you will be able to acceptsd and love all who are coming. Thank you for having responded to my call.

June 13, 1985   **Surrender to God and to me**

Dear children! Until the anniversary day I am calling you, the parish, to pray more and to let your prayer be a sign of surrender to God. Dear children, I know that you are all tired, but you don't know how to surrender yourselves to me. During these days surrender yourselves completely to me! Thank you for having responded to my call.

June 20, 1985   **Surrender to the Master of hearts and to me**

Dear children! For this Feast Day I wish to tell you to open your hearts to the Master of all hearts. Give me all your feelings and all your problems! I wish to comfort you in all your trials. I wish to fill you with peace, joy and love of God. Thank you for having responded to my call.

June 25, 1985 (Tuesday)   **Everyone also priest pray the rosary**

I invite you to call on everyone to pray the rosary. With the rosary you shall overcome all the adversities which Satan is trying to inflict on the Catholic church. All you priests, pray the rosary! Dedicate your time to the rosary! [This message Our Lady gave in response to the question of Marija Pavlović, *Our Lady, what do you wish to recommend to priests?*]

June 28, 1985 (Friday)   **Invitation to humility**

Dear children! Today I am giving you a message through which I desire to call you to humility. These days you have felt great joy because of all the people who have come and to whom you could tell your experiences with love. Now I invite you to continue in humility and with an open heart speak to all who are coming. Thank you for having responded to my message.

July 4, 1985   **Helping with confidence**

Dear children! I thank you for every sacrifice you have offered. And now I urge you to offer every sacrifice with love. I wish you, the helpless ones, to begin helping with confidence and the Lord will keep on giving to you in confidence. Thank you for having responded to my call.

July 11, 1985   **Protection from Satan**

Dear children! I love the parishs and with my mantle I protect it from every work of Satan. Pray that Satan retreats from the parish and from every individual who comes into the parish. In that way you shall be able to hear every call of God and answer it with your life. Thank you for having responded to my call.

July 18, 1985   **Blessed objects ward off Satan**

Dear children! Today I call you to place more blessed objects in your homes and that everyone put some blessed object on their person. Bless all the objects and thus Satan will attack you less because you will have armour against him. Thank you for having responded to my call.

July 25, 1985   **Obey my messages and live God's way**

Dear children! I desire to lead you, but you do not wish to listen to my messages. Today I am calling you to listen to the messages and then you will be able to live everything which God tells me to convey to you. Open yourselves to God and God will work through you and keep on giving you everything you need. Thank you for having responded to my call.

August 1, 1985   **A chosen and protected parish**

Dear children! I wish to tell you that I have chosen this parish and that I am guarding it in my hands like a little flower that does not want to die. I call you to surrender to me so that I can keep on presenting you to God, fresh and without sin. Satan has taken part of the plan and wants to possess it. Pray that he does not succeed in that, because I wish you for myself so I can keep on giving you to God. Thank you for having responded to my call.

August 8, 1985   **Conquer satan by the rosary**

Dear children! Today I call you especially now to advance against Satan by means of prayer. Satan wants to work still more now that you know he is at work. Dear children, put on the armour for battle and with the rosary in your hand defeat him! Thank you for having responded to my call.

August 15, 1985   **Solemn blessing of love**

Dear children! Today I am blessing you and I wish to tell you that I love you and that I urge you to live my messages. Today I am blessing you with the solemn blessing that the Alighty grants me. Thank you for having responded to my call.

August 22, 1985   **Love and trust God after overcoming temptation**

Dear children! Today I wish to tell you that God wants to send you trials which you can overcome by prayer. God is testing you through daily chores. Now pray to peacefully withstand every trial. From everything through which God tests you come out more open to God and approach Him with love. Thank you for having responded to my call.

August 29, 1985   **Foil Satan's plan to use the grapes**

Dear children! I am calling you to prayer! Especially since Satan wishes to take advantage of the yield of your vineyards. Pray that Satan does not succeed in his plan. Thank you for having responded to my call.

September 5, 1985   **Prayer has defeated Satan's plan**

Dear children! Today I thank you for all the prayers. Keep on praying all the more so that Satan will be far away from this place. Dear children, Satan's plan has failed. Pray for the fulfillment of what God plans in this parish. I especially thank the young people for the sacrifices they have offered up. Thank you for having responded to my call.

September 12, 1985   **The centrality of the cross**

Dear children! I wish to tell you that the cross should be central these days. Pray especially before the cross from which great graces are coming. Now in your homes make a special consecration to the cross. Promise that you will neither offend Jesus nor abuse the cross. Thank you for having responded to my call.

September 19, 1985   **No message was given by Our Lady**

September 20, 1985   **Spread the messages by living them**

Dear children! Today I invite you to live in humility all the messages which I am giving you. Do not become arrogant living the messages and saying 'I am living the messages'. If you shall bear and live the messages in your heart, everyone will feel it so that words, which serve those who do not obey, will not be necessary. For you, dear children, it is necessary to live and witness by your lives. Thank you for having responded to my call.

September 26, 1985   **Power of fasting for the plan of God**

Dear children! I thank you for all the prayers. Thank you for all the sacrifices. I wish to tell you, dear children, to renew the messages which I am giving you. Especially live the fast, because by fasting you will achieve and cause me the joy of the whole plan, which God is planning here in Medugorje, being fulfilled. Thank you for having responded to my call.

October 3, 1985   **Thank God for all the graces**

Dear children! I wish to tell you to thank God for all the graces which God has given you. For all the fruits thank the Lord and glorify Him! Dear children, learn to give thanks in little things and then you will be able to give thanks also for the big things. Thank you for having responded to my call.

October 10, 1985   **Messages lived are seed of holiness**

Dear children! I wish also today to call you to live the messages in the parish. Especially I wish to call the youth of the parish, who are dear to me. Dear children, if you live the message, you are living the seed of holiness. I, as the Mother, wish to call you all to holiness so that you can bestow it on others. You are a mirror to others! Thank you for having responded to my call.

October 17, 1985   **Work on cleaning your hearts**

Dear children! Everything has its own time. Today I call you to start working on your own hearts. Now that all the work in the field is over, you are finding time for cleaning even the most neglected areas, but you leave your heart aside. Work more and clean with love every part of your heart. Thank you for having responded to my call.

October 24, 1985   **Puting on the beauty of holiness**

Dear children! From day to day I wish to clothe you in holiness, goodness, obedience and God's love, so that from day to day you become more beautiful and more prepared for your Master. Dear children, listen to and live my messages. I wish to guide you. Thank you for having responded to my call.

October 31, 1985   **Do your share for the church**

Dear children! Today I wish to call you to work in the Church. I love all the same and I desire from each one to work as much as is possible. I know, dear children, that you can, but you do not wish to because you feel small and humble in these things. You need to be courageous and with little flowers do your share for the church and for Jesus so that everyone can be satisfied. Thank you for having responded to my call.

November 7, 1985   **Love can do all things**

Dear children! I am calling you to the love of neighbor and love toward the one from whom evil comes to you. In that way with love you will be able to discern the intentions of hearts. Pray and love, dear children! By love you are able to do even that which you think is impossible. Thank you for having responded to my call.

November 14, 1985   **A Mother's love for every child**

Dear children! I, your Mother, love you and wish to urge you to prayer. I am tireless, dear children, and I am calling you even then, when you are far away from my heart. I am a Mother, and evewn though I feel pain for each one who goes astray, I forgive easily and am happy for every child who returns to me. Thank you for having responded to my call.

November 21, 1985   **Show me your love by coming to Mass**

Dear children! I want to tell you that this season is especially for you from the parish. When it was summer, you saw that you have a lot of work. Now you don't have work in the fields, work on your own self personally! Come to Mass because this is the season given to you. Dear children, there are enough of those who come regularly despite bad weather because they love me and wish to show their love in a special way. What I want from you is to show me your love by coming to Mass, and the Lord will reward you abundantly. Thank you for having responded to my call.

November 28, 1985   **Come to prayer with awareness**

Dear children! I want to thank everyone for all you have done for me, especially the youth. I beseech you, dear children, come to prayer with awareness. In prayer you shall come to know the greatness of God. Thank you for having responded to my call.

December 5, 1985   Spiritual preparation for Christmas

Dear children! I am calling you to prepare yourselves for Christmas by means of penance, prayer and works of charity. Dear children, do not look toward material things, because then you will not be able to experience Christmas. Thank you for having responded to my call.

December 12, 1985   Glorifying Jesus for Christmas

Dear children! For Christmas my invitation in that together we glorify Jesus. I present Him to you in a special way on that day and my invitation to you is that on that day we glorify Jesus and His nativity. Dear children, on that day pray still more and think more about Jesus. Thank you for having responded to my call.

December 19, 1985   Special Christmas Day Blessings

Dear children! Today I wish to call you to love of neighbor. The more you will to love your neighbor, The more you shall experience Jesus especially on Christmas Day. God will bestow great gifts on you if you surrender yourselves to Him. I wish in a special way on Christmas Day to give mothers my own special motherly blessing, and Jesus will bless the rest with His own blessing. Thank you for having responded to my call.

December 26, 1985   I will lead you further in love

Dear children! I wish to thank all who have listened to my messages and who on Christmass Day have lived what I said. Undefiled by sin from now on, I wish to lead you further in love. Abandon your hearts to me! Thank you for having responded to my call.

January 2, 1986   Decide completely for God

Dear children! I call you to decide completely for God. I beseech you, dear children, to surrender yourselves completely and you shall be able to live everything I am telling you, It shall not be difficult for you to surrender yourselves completely to God. Thank you for having responded to my call.

January 9, 1986   Help Jesus' plans by prayer

Dear children! I call you by your prayers to help Jesus along in the fulfilment of all the plans which He is forming here. And offer your sacrifices to Jesus in order that everything is fulfilled that way He has planned it and that Satan can accomplish nothing. Thank you for having responded to my call.

January 16, 1986   I need your prayers for God's glory

Dear children! Today also I am callign you to prayer. Your prayers are necessary to me so that God may be glorified through all of you. Dear children, I pray you, obey and live the Mother's invitation, because only out of love am I calling you in order that I might help you. Thank you for having responded to my call.

January 23, 1986   Beg conversion for your neighbour

Dear children! Again I call you to prayer with the heart. If you pray with the heart, dear children, the ice of your brothers will melt and every barrier shall disappear. Conversion will be easy for all who desire to accept it. That is the gift which by prayer you must obtain for your neighbour. Thank you for having responded to my call.

January 30, 1986   As an image of Mary make her present

Dear children! Today I call you to pray that God's plans for us may be realized and also everything that God desires through you! Help others to be converted, especially those who are coming to Medugorje. Dear children, do not allow Satan to get control of your hearts, so you would be an image of Satan and not of me. I call you to pray for how you might be witnesses of my presence. Without you, God cannot bring to reality that which He desires. God has given a free will to everyone, and its in your control. Thank you for having responded to my call.

February 6, 1986   The Parish is specially chosen and responsible

Dear children! This parish, which I have chosen, is special and different from others. And I am giving great graces to all who pray with the heart. Dear children, I am giving the messages first of all to the residents of the parish, and then to all the others. First of all you must accept the messages, and then the others. You shall be answerable to me and to my Son, Jesus. Thank you for having responded to my call.

February 13, 1986   During Lent renounce useless things

Dear children! This Lent is a special incentive for you to change. Start from this moment. Turn off the television and renounce various things that are of no value. Dear children, I am calling you individually to conversion. This season is for you. Thank you for having responded to my call.

February 20, 1986   Special graces given before the Cross

Dear children! The second message of these Lenten days is that you renew prayer before the cross. Dear children, I am giving you special graces and Jesus is giving you special gifts from the cross. Take them and live! Reflect on Jesus' Passion and in your life be united with Jesus! Thank you for having responded to my call.

February 27, 1986   Live the messages in humility

Dear children! In humility live the messages which I am giving you. Thank you for having responded to my call.

March 6, 1986   Bestill more open to God

Dear children! Today I call you to open yourselves more to God, so that He can work through you. The more you open yourselves, the more you receive the fruits. I wish to call you again to prayer. Thank you for having responded to my call.

March 13, 1986   **Help me with your sacrifices**

Dear children! Today I call you to live Lent by means of your little sacrifices. Thank you for every sacrifice you have brought me. Dear children, live that way continuously, and with your love help me to present the sacrifice. God will reward you for that. Thank you for having responded to my call.

March 20, 1986   **Success comes only through prayer**

Dear children! Today I call you to approach prayer actively. You wish to live everything I am telling you, but you are not suceeding because you are not praying. Dear children, I beseech you to open yourselves and begin to pray. Prayer will be your joy. If you make a start, it won't be boring to you because you will be praying out of joy. Thank you for having responded to my call.

March 27, 1986   **Love is the greatest necessity**

Dear children! I wish to thank you for all the sacrifices and I invite you to the greatest sacrifice, the sacrifice of love. Without love, you are not able to accept either me or my Son. Without love, you cannot give an account of your experiences to others. Therefore, dear children, I call you to begin to live love within yourselves. Thank you for having responded to my call.

April 3, 1986   **Live the Holy Mass**

Dear children! I wish to call you to a living of the Holy Mass. There are many of you who have sensed the beauty of the Holy Mass, but there are also those who come unwillingly. I have chosen you, dear children, but Jesus gives you His graces in the Mass. Therefore, consciously live the Holy Mass and let your coming to it be a joyful one. Come to it with love and make the Mass your own. Thank you for having responded to my call.

April 10, 1986   **To grow in love you need God's blessing**

Dear children! I desire to call you to grow in love. A flower is not able to grow normally without water. So also you, dear children, are not able to grow without God's blessing. From day to day you need to seek His blessing so you will grow normally and perform all your actions in union with God. Thank you for having responded to my call.

April 17, 1986   **Gifts of the Holy Spirit are necessary**

Dear children! You are absorbed with material things, but in the material you lose everything that God wishes to give you. I call you, dear children, to pray for the gifts of the Holy Spirit which are necessary for you now in order to be able to give witness to my presence here and to all that I am giving you. Dear children, let go to me so I can lead you completely. Don't be absorbed with material things. Thank you for having responded to my call.

April 24, 1986   **Everyone is important**

Dear children! Today my invitation is that you pray. Dear children, you are forgetting that you are all important. The elderly are especially important in the family. Urgew them to pray. Let all the young people be an example to others by their life and let them witness to Jesus. Dear children, I beseech you, begion to change through prayer and you will know what you need to do. Thank you for having responded to my call.

May 1, 1986   **Let every family be active in prayer**

Dear children! I beseech you to start changing you life in the family. Let the family be a harmonious flower that I wish to give to Jesus. Dear children, let every family be active in prayer for I wish that the fruits in the family be seen one day. Only that way shall I give you all, like petals, as a gift to Jesus in fulfilment of God's plans. Thank you for having responded to my call.

May 8, 1986   **You all share responsibility for the messages**

Dear children! You are the ones responsible for the messages. The source of grace is here, but you, dear children, are the vessels which transport the gifts. Therefore, dear children, I am calling you to do your job with responsibility. Each one shall be responsible according to his own ability. Dear children, I am calling you to give the gifts to others with love, and not to keep them for yourselves. Thank you for having responded to my call.

May 15, 1986   **Give me your heart and you can respond**

Dear children! Today I call you to give me your heart so I can change it to be like mine. You are wondering, dear children, why you cannot respond to that which I am seeking from you. You are not able to because you have not given me your heart so I can change it. You are talking but you are not doing. I call on you to do everything that I am telling you. That way I will be with you. Thank you for having responded to my call.

May 22, 1986   **I want you to know how much I love you**

Dear children! Today I wish to give you my own love. You do not know, dear children, how greats my love is, and you do not know how to accept it. In various ways I wish to show it to you, but you, dear children, do not recognise it. You do not understand my words with your heart and neither are you able to comprehend my love. Dear children, accept me in your life and so you will be able to accept all I am saying to you and to which I am calling you. Thank you for having responded to my call.

May 29, 1986   **Ardent love toward God and neighbour**

Dear children! Today my call to you is that in your life you live toward God and neighbour. Without love, dear children, you can do nothing. Therefore, dear children, I am calling you to live in mutual love. Only in that way will you be able to love and accept both me and all those around you who are coming into your parish. Everyone will sense my love through you. Therefore, I beseech you, dear children, to start loving from today with an ardent love, the love with which I love you. Thank you for having responded to my call.

June 5, 1986   Be the Light of Jesuss in the world

Dear children! Today I am calling on you to decide whether or not you wish to live the messages which I am giving you. I wish you to be active in living and spreading the messages. Especially, dear children, I wish that you all be the reflection of Jesus, which will enlighten this unfaithful world walking in darkness. I wish all of you to be the light for everyone and that you give witness in the light. Dear children, you are not called to the darkness, but you are called to the light. Therefore, live the light with your own life. Thank you for having responded to my call.

June 12, 1986   The Rosary, a joyful obligation

Dear children! Today I call you to begin to pray the Rosary with a living faith. That way I will be able to help you. You, dear children, wish to obtain graces, but you are not praying. I am not able to help you because you do not want to get started. Dear children, I am calling you to pray the Rosary and that your Rosary be an obligation which you shall fulfill with joy. That way you shall understand the reason I am with you this long. I desire to teach you to pray. Thank you for having responded to my call.

June 19, 1986   Unceasing prayer brings joy even
                                                                  to sufferings

Dear children! During these days my Lord is allowing me to be able to intercede more graces for you. Therefore, I wish to urge you once more to pray, dear children! Pray without ceasing! That way I will give you the joy which the Lord gives to me. With these graces, dear children, I want your sufferings to be a joy. I am your Mother and I desire to help you. Thank you for having responded to my call.

June 26, 1986   Protect this oasis of peace and prayer

Dear children! God is allowing me along with Himself to bring abouts this oasis of peace. I wish to call on you to protect it and that the oasis always be unspoiled. There are those who by their carelessness are destroying the peace and the prayer. I am inviting you to give witness and by your own life to help to preserve the peace. Thank you for having responded to my call.

July 3, 1986   Keep prayer in the first place

Dear children! I am calling you all to prayer. Without prayer, dear children, you are not able to experience either God, or me or the graces which I am giving you. Therefore, my call to you is that the beginning and end of your day always be prayer. Dear children, I wish to lead you daily more and more in prayer, but you are not able to grow because you do not desire it. My call, dear children, is that for you prayer be in the first place. Thank you for having responded to my call.

July 10, 1986   Holiness is overcoming with love

Dear children! Today I am calling you to holiness. Without holiness you cannot live. Therefore, with love overcome every sin and with love overcome all the difficulties which are coming to you. Dear children, I beseech you to live love within yourselves. Thank you for having responded to my call.

July 17, 1986   I am Mediartrix between you and God

Dear children! Today I am calling you to reflect upon why I am with you this long. I am the Mediatrix between you and God. Therefore, dear children, I desire to call you to live always out of love all that which God desires of you. For that reason, dear children, in your own humility live all the messages which I am giving you. Thank you for having responded to my call.

July 24, 1986   Help all to live in holiness

Dear children! I rejoice because of all of you who are on the way of holiness and I beseech you, by your own testimony help those who do not know how to live in holiness. Therefore, dear children, let your family be a place where holiness is born. Help everyone to live in holiness, but especially your own family. Thank you for having responded to my call.

July 31, 1986   Always bring harmony, peace and love

Dear children! Hatred gives birth to dissensions and does not regard anyone or anything. I call you always to bring harmony and peace. Especially, dear children, in the place where you live, act with love. Let your only instrument always be love. By love turn everything into good which Satan desires to destroy and possess. Only that way shall you be completely mine and I shall be able to help you. Thank you for having responded to my call.

August 7, 1986   Satan lurks by the oasis of peace

Dear children! You know that I promised you an oasis of peace, but you don't know that beside an oasis stands the desert, where Satan is lurking and wanting to tempt each one of you. Dear children, only by prayer are you able to overcome every influence of Satan in your place. I am with you, but I cannot take away your freedom. Thank you for having responded to my call.

August 14, 1986   Joyful encounter with the Lord in prayer

Dear children! My call to you is that your prayer be the joy of an encounter with the Lord. I am not able to guide you as long as you yourselves do not experience joy in prayer. From day to day I desire to lead you more and more in prayer, but I do not wish to force you. Thank you for having responded to my call.

August 21, 1986   I pray daily for you to understand my love

Dear children! I thank you for the love which you are showing me. You know, dear children, that I love you immeasurably and daily I pray the Lord to help you to understand the love which I am showing you. Therefore, you, dear children, pray, pray, pray!

August 28, 1986   I need you to help the world

Dear children! My call is that in everything you would be an image for others, especially in prayer and witnessing. Dear children, without you I am not able to help the world. I desire that you cooperate with me in everything, even in the smallest things. Therefore, dear children, help me by letting your prayer be from the heart and all of you surrendering completely to me. That way I shall be able to teach and lead you on this way which I have begun with you. Thank you for having responded to my call.

September 4, 1986 **I can foil Satan with your help**

Dear children! Today again I am calling you to prayer and fasting. You know, dear children, that with your help I am able to accomplish everything and force Satan not to be seducing to evil and to remove himselfs from this place. Dear children, Satan is lurking for each individual. Especially in everyday affairs he wants to spread confusion among each one of you. Therefore, dear children, my call to you is that your day would be only prayer and complete surrender to God. Thank you for having responded to my call.

September 11, 1986 **The cross to be a joy for you**

Dear children! For these days while you are joyfully celebrating the cross, I desire that your cross also would be a joy for you. Especially, dear children, pray that you may be able to accept sickness and suffering with love the way Jesus accepted them. Only that way shall I be able with joy to give out to you the graces and healings which Jesus is permitting me. Thank you for having responded to my call.

September 18, 1986 **I need your sacrifices to help you**

Dear children! Today again I thank you for all that you have accomplished for me in these days. Especially, dear children, I thank you in the Name of Jesuss for the sacrifices which you offered in this past week. Dear children, you are forgetting that I desire sacrifices from you so I can help you and drive Satan away from you. Therefore, I am calling you again to offer sacrifices with a special reverence toward God. Thank you for having responded to my call.

September 25, 1986 **Let truth prevail in all hearts**

Dear children! By your own peace I am calling you to help others to see and begin to seek peace. You, dear children, are at peace and not able to comprehend nonpeace. Therefore, I am calling you, so that by your prayer and your life you help to destroy everythings that's evil in people and uncover the deception that Satan makes use of. You pray that the truth prevails in all hearts. Thank you for having responded to my call.

October 2, 1986 **Unconditional commitment to prayer**

Dear children! Today again I am calling you to pray. You, dear children, are not able to understand how great the value of prayer is as long as you yourselves do not say: 'now is the time for prayer, now nothing else is important to me, now not one person is important to me but God'. Dear children, consecrate yourselves to prayer with a special love so that God will be able to render graces back to you. Thank you for having responded to my call.

October 9, 1986 **I want each individual to be holy**

Dear children! You know that I desire to lead you on the way of holiness, but I do not want to compel you to be saints by force. I desire that each of you by your own little self-denials help yourself and me so I can lead you from day to day closer to holiness. Therefore, dear children, I do not desire to force you to observe the messages. But rather this long time that I am with you is a sign that I love you immeasurably and what I desire of each individual is to become holy. Thank you for having responded to my call.

October 16, 1986 **Resist Satan by complete surrender to God**

Dear children! Today again I want to show you how much I love you, but I am sorry that I am not able to help each one to understand my love. Therefore, dear children, I am calling you to prayer and complete surrender to God, because Satan wants to sift you through everyday affairs and in your life he wants to snatch the first place. Therefore, dear children, pray without ceasing! Thank you for having responded to my call.

October 23, 1986 **By prayer realize what God is giving you**

Dear children! Today again I call you to pray. Especially, dear children, do I call you to pray for peace. Without your prayers, dear children, I cannot help you to fulfill the message which the Lord has given me to give to you. Therefore, dear children, pray, so that in prayer you realize what God is giving you. Thank you for having responded to my call.

October 30, 1986 **Take the messages seriously and live them**

Dear children! Today again I desire to call you to take seriously and carry out the messages which I am giving you. Dear children, it is for your sake that I have stayed this long so I could help you to fulfill all the messages which I am giving you. Therefore, dear children, out of love for me carry out all the messages which I am giving you. Thank you for having responded to my call.

November 6, 1986 **Make friends of the sould in purgatory**

Dear children! Today I wish to call you to pray daily for the souls in purgatory. For every soul prayer and grace is necessary to reach God and the love of God. By doing this, dear children, you obtain new intercessors who will help you in life to realize that all the earthly things are not important for you, that only Heaven is that for which it is necessary to strive. Therefore, dear children, pray without ceasing that you may be able to help yourselves and the others to whom your prayers will bring joy. Thank you for having responded to my call.

November 13, 1986 **Obtain holiness from this source of grace**

Dear children! Today again I am calling you to pray with your whole heart and day by day to change your life. Especially, dear children, I am calling that by your prayers and sacrifices you begin to live in holiness, because I desire that each one of you who has been to this fountain of grace will come to Paradise with the special gift which you shall give me, and that is holiness. Therefore, dear children, pray and daily change your life in order to become holy. I shall always be close to you. Thank you for having responded to my call.

November 20, 1986 **Let love prevail in all of you**

Dear children! Today also I am calling you to live and follow with a special love all the messages which I am giving you. Dear children, God does not want you lukewarm and undecided, but that you totally surrender to Him. You know that I love you and that out of love I long for you. Therefore, dear children, you also decide for love so that you will long for and daily experience God's love. Dear children, decide for love so that love prevails in all of you, but not human love, rather God's love. Thank you for having responded to my call.

November 27, 1986   **Consecrate your life to me**

Dear children! Again today I call you to consecrate your life to me with love, so I am able to guide you with love. I love you, dear children, with a special love and I desire to bring you all to Heaven unto God. I want you to realize that this life lasts briefly compared to the one in Heaven. Therefore, dear children, decide again today for God. Only that way will I be able to show how much you are dear to me and how much I desire all to be saved and to be with me in Heaven. Thank you for having responded to my call.

December 4, 1986   •   **Prepare especially for Christmas**

Dear children! Today I call you to prepare your hearts for these days when the Lord particularlys desires to purify you from all the sins of your past. You, dear children, are not able by yourselves, therefore I am here to help you. You pray, dear children! Only that way shall you be able to recognize all the evil that is in you and surrender it to the Lord so the Lord may completely purify your hearts. Therefore, dear children, pray without ceasing and prepare your hearts in penance and fasting. Thank you for having responded to my call.

December 11, 1986   **Experiencing the joy of the new-born Jesus**

Dear children! I am calling you to pray especially at this time in order to experience the joy of meeting with the new-born Jesus. Dear children, I desire that you experience these days just as I experience them. With joy I wish to guide you and show you the joy into which I desire to bring each one of you. Therefore, dear children, pray and surrender completely to me. Thank you for having responded to my call.

December 18, 1986   **Transforming power of prayer**

Dear children! Once again I desire to call you to prayer. When you pray you are much more beautiful, like flowers, which after the snow, show all their beauty and all their colors become indescribable. So also you, dear children, after prayer show before God all so much more what is beautiful and are you beloved by Him. Therefore dear children, pray and open your inner self to the Lord so that He makes of you a harmonious and beautiful flower for Paradise. Thank you for having responded to my call.

December 25, 1986, Christmas Day — **Special graces to open hearts**

*D*ear children! Today also I give thanks to the Lord for all that He is doing for me, especially for this gift that I am able to be with you also today. Dear children, these are the days in which the Father grants special graces to all who open their hearts. I bless you and I desire that you too, dear children, become alive to the graces and place everything at God's disposal so that He may be glorified through you. My heart carefully follows your progress. Thank you for having responded to my call.

January 1, 1987 — **Pray unceasingly and live my messages**

*D*ear children! Today I wish to call on all of you that in the New Year you live the messages which I am giving you. Dear children, you know that for your sake I have remained a long time so I might teach you how to make progress in the way of holiness. Therefore, dear children, pray without ceasing and live the messages which I am giving you for I am doing it with great love toward God and toward you. Thank you for having responded to my call.

January 8, 1987 — **The time has been fulfilled**

*D*ear children! I desire to thank you for every response to the messages. Especially, dear children, thank you for all the sacrifices and prayers which you have presented to me. Dear children, I desire to keep on giving you still further messages, only not every Thursday, dear children, but on each 25th in the month. The time has come when what my Lord desired has been fulfilled. Now I will give you less messages, but I am still with you. Therefore, dear children, I beseech you, listen to my messages and live them, so I can guide you. Dear children, thank you for having responded to my call.

THE MONTHLY MESSAGES OF OUR LADY

January 25, 1987　　　　　　　You have a role in God's great plan

Dear children! Behold, also today I want to call you to start living a new life as of today. Dear children, I want you to comprehend that God has chosen each one of you, in order to use you in His great plan for the salvation of mankind. You are not able to comprehend how great your role is in God's design. Therefore, dear children, pray so that in prayer you may be able to comprehend what God's plan is in your regard. I am with you in order that you may be able to bring it about in all its fullness. Thank you for having responded to my call.

February 25, 1987　　　　　　The way of conversion, a way of joy

Dear children! Today I want to wrap you all in my mantle and lead you all along the way of conversion. Dear children, I beseech you, surrender to the Lord your entire past, all the evil that has accumulated in your hearts. I want each one of you to be happy, but in sin nobody can be happy. Therefore, dear children, pray, and in prayer you shall realize a new way of joy. Joy will manifest in your hearts and thus you shall be joyful witnesses of that which I am My Son want from each one of you. I am blessing you. Thank you for having responded to my call.

March 25, 1987　　　　　　The new life excludes committing sin

Dear children! Today I am grateful to you for your presence in this place, where I am giving you special graces. I call each one of you to begin to live as of today that life which God wishes of you and to begin to perform good works of love and mercy. I do not want you, dear children, to live the message and be committing sin which is displeasing to me. Therefore, dear children, I want each of you to live a new life without destroying all that God produces in you and is giving you. I give you my special blessing and I am remaining with you on your way of conversion. Thank you for having responded to my call.

April 25, 1987　　　　　　　　　Prayer with the heart

Dear children! Today also I am calling you to prayer. You know, dear children, that God grants special grace in prayer. Therefore, seek and pray in order that you may be able to comprehend all that I am giving here. I call you, dear children, to prayer with the heart. You know that without prayer you cannot comprehend all that God is planning throughd each one of you. Therefore, pray! I desire that through each one of you God's plan may be fulfilled, that all which God has planted in your heart may keep on growing. So pray that God's blessing may protect each one of you from all the evil that is threatening you. I bless you, dear children. Thank you for having responded to my call.

May 25, 1987　　　　　　　　　Start living in God's love

Dear children! I am calling every one of you to start living in God's love. Dear children, you are ready to commit sin, and to put yourselves in the hands of Satan without reflecting. I call on each one of you to consciously

decide for God and against Satan. I am your Mother and, therefore, I want to lead you all to perfect holiness. I want each one of you to be happy here on earth and to be with me in Heaven. That is, dear children, the purpose of my coming here and it's my desire. Thank you for having responded to my call.

June 25, 1987　　　　　　　Live in the peace which God gives

Dear children! Today I thank you and I wants to invite you all to God's peace. I want each one of you to experience in your heart that peace which God gives. I want to bless you all today. I am blessing you with God's blessing and I beseech you, dear children, to follow and to live my way. I love you, dear children, and so not even counting the numbewr of times, I go on calling you and I thank you for all that you are doing for my intentions. I beg you, help me to present you to God and to save you. Thank you for having responded to my call.

July 25, 1987　　　　　　　　Take up the way of holiness

Dear children! I beseech you to take up the way of holiness beginning today. I love you and, therefore, I want you to be holy. I do not want Satan to block you on that way. Dear children, pray and accept all that God is offering you on a way which is bitter. But at the same time, God willreveal every sweetness to whomever begins to go on that way, and he will gladly answer every call of God. Do not attribute importance to petty things. Long for heaven. Thank you for having responded to my call.

August 25, 1987　　　　　　　Decide to live my messages

Dear children! Today also I am calling you all in order that each one of you decides to live my messages. God has permitted me also in this year, which the Church has dedicated to me, to be able to speak to you and to be able to spur you on to holiness. Dear children, seek from God the graces which He is giving you through me. I am ready to intercede with God for all that you seek so that your holiness may be complete. Therefore, dear children, do not forget to seek, because God has permitted me to obtain graces for you. Thank you for having responded to my call.

September 25, 1987　　　　　　　Let prayer be your life

Dear children! Today also I want to call you all to prayer. Let prayer be your life. Dear children, dedicate your time only to Jesus and He will give you everything that you are seeking. He will reveal Himself to you in fulness. Dear children, Satan is strong and is waiting to test each one of you. Pray, and that way he will neither be able to injure you nor block you on the way of holiness. Dear children, through prayer grow all the mores toward God from day to day. Thank you for having responded to my call.

October 25, 1987　　　　　　　　　Decide for Paradise

Dear children! Today I want to call you all of you to decide for Paradise. The way is difficult for those who have not decided for God. Dear children, decide and believe that God is offering Himself to you in His fullness. You are invited and you need to answer the call of the Father, who is calling you through me. Pray, because in prayer each one of you will be able to achieve complete love. I am blessing you and I desire to help you so that each one of you might be under my motherly mantle. Thank you for having responded to my call.

November 25, 1987   **Surrender everything to me**

Dear children! Today also I call each one of you to decide to surrender again everything completely to me. Only that way will I be able to present each of you to God. Dear children, you know that I love you immeasurably and that I desire each of you for myself, but God has given to all a freedom which I lovingly respect and humbly submit to. I desire, dear children, that you help so that everything God has planned in this parish shall be realized. If you do not pray, you shall not be able to recognize my love and the plans which God has for this parish and for each individual. Pray that Satan does not entice you with his pride and deceptive strength. I am with you and I want you to believe me, that I love you. Thank you for having responded to my call.

December 25, 1987   **Rejoice with me because of Jesus**

Dear children! Rejoice with me! My heart is rejoicing because of Jesus and today I want ti give Him to you. Dear children, I want each one of you to pen your heart to Jesus and I will give Him to you with love. Dear children, I want Him to change you, to teach you and to protect you. Today I am praying in a special way for each one of you and I am presenting you to God so He will manifest Himself in you. I am calling you to sincere prayer with the heart so that every prayer of yours may be an encounter with God. In your work and in your everyday life, put God in the first place. I call you today with great seriousness to obey me and to do as I am calling you. Thank you for having responded to my call.

January 25, 1988   **Call to complete conversion**

Dear children! Today again I am calling you to complete conversion, which is difficult for those who have not chosen God. I am calling you, dear children, to convert fully to God. God can give you everything that you seek from Him. but you seek God only when sicknesses, problems and difficulties come to you and you think that God is far from you and is not listening and does not hear your prayers. No, dear children, that is not the truth! When you are far from God, you cannot receive graces because you do not seek them with a firm faith. Day by day I am praying for you and I want to draw you ever closer to God, but I cannot if you don't want. Therefore, dear children, put your life in God's hands. I bless you all. Thank you for having responded to my call.

February 25, 1988   **Prayer and complete surrender to God**

Dear children! Today again I am calling you to prayer and complete surrender to God. You know that I love you and am coming here out of love, so I could show you the path of peace and salvation for your souls. I want you to obey me and not permit Satan to seduce you. Dear children, Satan is very strong and, therefore, I ask you to dedicate your prayers to me so that those who are under his influence may be saved. Give witness by your life, sacrifice your lives for the salvation of the world. I am with you and I am grateful to you, but in heaven you shall receive the Father's reward which He has promised you. Therefore, little children, do not be afraid. If you pray, Satan cannot injure you even a little, because you are God's children and He is watching over you. Pray, and let the rosary always be in your hands as a sign to Satan that you belong me. Thank you for having responded to my call.

March 25, 1988   **Complete surrender to God**

Dear children! Today also I am calling you to a complete surrender to God. You, dear children, are not conscious of how God loves you with such a great love. Because of it He permits me to be with you so I can instruct you and help you to find the way of peace. That way, however, you cannot discover if you do not pray. Therefore, dear children, forsake everything and consecrate your time to God and then God will bestow gifts upon you and bless you. Little children, do not forget that your life is fleeting like the spring flower which today is wondrously beautiful, but tomorrow has vanished. Therefore, pray in such a way that your prayer, your surrender to God may become like a road sign. That way your witness will not only have value for yourselves, but for all of eternity. Thank you for having responded to my call.

April 25, 1988   **Holiness means complete surrender**

Dear children! God wants to make you holy. Therefore, through me He is calling you to complete surrender. Let the Holy Mass be your life. Understand that the church is God's palace, the place in which I gather you and want to show you the way to God. Come and pray! Neither look to others nor slander them, but rather let your life be a testimony on the way of holiness. Churches deserve respect and are set apart as holy because God, who became Man, dwells in them day and night. Therefore, little children, believe and pray that the Father increase your faith, and then ask for whatever you need. I am with you and I rejoice because of your conversion and I am protecting you with my motherly mantle. Thank you for having responded to my call.

May 25, 1988   **Complete surrender to God's love conquers the world**

Dear children! I am calling you to a complete surrender to God. Pray, little children, than Satan does not sway you like branches in the wind. Be strong in God. I desire that through you the whole world may get to know the God of joy. Neither be anxious nor worried. God will help you and show you the way. I want you to love all men with my love, both the good and the bad. Only that way will love conquer the world. Little children, you are mine. I love you I want you to surrender to me so I can lead you to God. Pray without ceasing so that Satan cannot take advantage of you. Pray so that you realize that you are mine. I bless you with the blessing of joy. Thank you for having responded to my call.

June 25, 1988   **The love that is loyal and pleasing to God**

Dear children! Today I am calling you to the love which is loyal and pleasing to God. Little children, love bears everything bitter and difficult for the sake of Jesus who is love. Therefore, dear children, pray God to come to your aid, not, however, according to your desires but according to His love. Surrender yourselves to God so that He may heal you, console you, and forgive everything inside you which is a hindrance on the way of love. In this way God can mould your life and you will grow in love. Dear children, glorify god with the canticle of love so that God's love may be able to grow in you day by day to its fullness. Thank you for having responded to my call.

July 25, 1988   **Complete surrender to God as King**

Dear children! Today I am calling you to a complete surrender to God. Everything you do and everything you possess give over to God so that He can take control in your life as King of all that you possess. That way through me God can lead you into the depths of the spiritual life. Little children, do not be afraid because I am with you even when you think there is no way out and that Satan is in control. I am bringing peace to you. I am your Mother and the Queen of Peace. I am blessing you with the blessing of joy so that for you God may be everything in life. Thank you for having responded to my call.

August 25, 1988   **Rejoicing in God the Creator**

Dear children! Today I invite you all to rejoice in the life which God gives you. Little children, rejoice in God the Creator because He has created you so wonderfully. Pray that your life be a joyful thanksgiving, which flows out of your heart like a river of joy. Little children, give thanks unceasingly for all that you possess, for each little gift, which God has given you so that a joyful blessing always comes down from God upon your life. Thank you for having responded to my call.

September 25, 1988   **All for holiness without exception**

Dear children! Today I am calling all of you without exception to the way of holiness in your life. God gave you the gift of holiness. Pray that you may more and more comprehend it and in that way you will be able by your life to bear witness for God. Dear children, I am blessing you and I intercede for you to God so that your way and your witness may be a complete one and a joy for God. Thank you for having responded to my call.

October 25, 1988   **Consecration to Jesus and Mary**

Dear children! My call on you that you live the messages which I am giving you is a daily one. Especially, little children, because I want to draw you closer to the Heart of Jesus. Therefore, little children, I am calling you today to the prayer of Consecration to my Immaculate Heart. I want you to consecrate yourselves as persons, families and parsihes so that all belongs to God through my hands. Therefore, dear little children, pray that you may comprehend the greatness of this message which I am giving you. I do not want anything for myself, rather all for the salvation of your souls. Satan is strong and, therefore, you little children by constant prayer press tightly to my motherly heart. Thank you for having responded to my call.

November 25, 1988   **Meeting God the Creator in daily prayer**

Dear children! I am calling you to prayer so that in prayer you have an encounter with God. God is offering and giving Himself to you. But He seeks from you that you answer His call in your freedom. Therefore, little children, set a time during the day when you can pray in peace and humility and meet with God the Creator. I am with you and I intercede with God for you. So be on watch that every encounter in prayer be a joyful meeting with God. Thank you for having responded to my call.

December 25, 1988   **Live peace in your hearts and surroundings**

Dear children! I am calling you to peace. Live peace in your heart and in your surroundings, so that all may recognize the peace, which does not come from you, but from God. Little children, today is a great day. Rejoice with me! Celebrate the birth of Jesus with my peace, the peace with which I came as your Mother, Queen of Peace. Today I am giving you my special blessing. Carry it to every creature so that each one may have peace. Thank you for having responded to my call.

January 25, 1989   **The beauty and greatness of holiness**

Dear children! Today I am calling you to the way of holiness. Pray that you may comprehend the beauty and the greatness of this way, where God reveals Himself to you in a special way. Pray that you may be open to everything that God is doing through you and that in your life you may be enabled to give thanks to God and to rejoice over everything that He is doing through each individual. I am giving you my blessing. Thank you for having responded to my call.

February 25, 1989   **In Lent be united with Jesus**

Dear children! Today I am calling you to prayer of the heart. Throughout this season of grace I desire each of you to be united with Jesus, but without unceasing prayer you cannot experience the beauty and greatness of the grace which God is offering you. Therefore, little children, at all times fill your heart with even the smallest prayers. I am with you and unceasingly I keep watch over every heart which is given to me. Thank you for having responded to my call.

March 25, 1989   **Invited to holiness but still far away**

Dear children! I am calling you to a complete surrender to God. I am calling you to great joy and peace which only God can give. I am with you and I intercede for you everyday before God. I call you, little children, to listen to me and to live the messages which I am giving you. Already for years yu are invited to holiness, but you are still far away. I am blessing you. Thank you for having responded to my call.

April 25, 1989   **Discover God in everything!**

Dear children! I am calling you to a complete surrender to God. Let everything that you possess be in the hands of God. Only in that way shall you have joy in your heart. Little children, rejoice in everything that you have. And give thanks to God because everything is God's gift to you. That way in your life you shall be able to give thanks for everything and discover God in everything, even in the smallest flower. You shall discover joy. You shall discover God. Thank you for having responded to my call.

May 25, 1989   **Discover the greatness and joy of life**

Dear children! I am calling you to openness to God. You see, little children, how nature is opening herself and is giving life and fruits. In the same way, I am calling you to a life with God and a complete surrender to Him. Little children, I am with you and unceasingly I desire to lead you into the joy of life. I desire that each one of you discovers the joy and the love which is found only in God and which only God can give. God wants nothing else from you but your surrender. Therefore, little children, decide seriously for God, because everything else passes away. God alone does not pass away. Pray that you may discover the greatness and the joy of life which God is giving you. Thank you for having responded to my call.

June 25, 1989   **Eight years of graces for each one**

Dear children! Today I call you to live the messages which I have been giving you during the past eight years. This is a time of graces and I desire that the grace of God be great for every single one of you. I am blessing you and I love you with a special love. Thank you for having responded to my call.

July 25, 1989   **Daily encounter with God in silence**

Dear children! Today I am calling you to renew your heart. Open yourselves to God and surrender to Him all your difficulties and crosses so God may turn everything into joy. Little children, you cannot open yourselves to God if you do not pray. Therefore, from today decide to consecrate a time in the day only for an encounter with God in silence. In that way you will be able with God to witness my presence here. Little children, I do not wish to force you, rather freely give God your time like children of God. Thank you for having responded to my call.

August 25, 1989   **Prayer to rule in the whole world**

Dear children! I call you to prayer. By means of prayer, little children, you obtain joy and peace. Through prayer you are richer in the grace of God. Therefore, little children, let prayer be the life of each one of you. Especially I call you to pray that all those who are far away from God may be converted. Then our hearts shall be richer because God will rule in the hearts of all men. Therefore, little children, pray, pray, pray! Let prayer begin to rule in the whole world! Thank you for having responded to my call.

September 25, 1989   **Rejoicing in God's gifts**

Dear children! Today I invite you to give thanks to God for all the gifts that you have discovered in the course of your life, and even for the least gift that you have perceived. I give thanks with you and want all of you to experience the joy of these gifts, and I want God to be everything for each one of you. And then, little children, you can grow continuously on the way of holiness. Thank you for having responded to my call.

October 25, 1989   **Decide seriously for God**

Dear children! Today also I am inviting you to prayer. I am always inviting you, but you are still far away. Therefore, from today, decide seriously to dedicate time to God. I am with you and I wish to teach you to pray with the heart. In prayer with the heart you shall encounter God. Therefore, little children, pray, pray, pray! Thank you for having responded to my call.

November 25, 1989

Dear children! I am inviting you for years by these messages which I am giving you. Little children, by means of the messages I wish to make a very beautiful mosaic in your hearts so I might be able to present each one of you to God like the original image. Therefore, little children, I desire that your decisions be free before God, because He has given you freedom. Therefore, pray so that, free from any influence of Satan, you may decide only for God. I am praying for you before God and I am seeking your surrender to God. Thank you for having responded to my call.

December 25, 1989

Dear children! Today I am blessing you in a special way with my motherly blessing and I am interceding for you before God that He give you the gift of conversion of the heart. For years I am calling you and exhorting you to a deep spirituals life in simplicity, but you are so cold. Therefore, little children, I ask you to accept and live the messages with seriousness, so that your soul will not be sad when I will no longer be with you, and when I will no longer lead you like insecure children in their first steps. Therefore, little children, each day read the messages which I have given you and transform them into life. I love you and, therefore, I am calling you all to the way of salvation with God. Thank you for having responded to my call.

January 25, 1990

Dear children! Today I invite you to decide for God once again and to choose Him before everything and above everything, so that He may work miracles in your life and that day by day your life may become joy with Him. Therefore, little children, pray and do not permit Satan to work in your life through misunderstandings, not-understanding and not-accepting one another. Pray that you may be able to comprehend the greatness and the beauty of the gift of life. Thank you for having responded to my call.

February 25, 1990

Dear children! I invite you to surrender to God. In this season I especially want you to renounce all the things to which you are attached but are hurting your spiritual life. Therefore, little children, decide completely for God, and do not allow Satan to come into your life through those things that hurt both you and your spiritual life. Little children, God is offering Himself to you in fullness, and you can discover and know Him only in prayer. Therefore, make a decision for prayer! Thank you for having responded to my call.

March 25, 1990

Dear children! I am with you even if you are not conscious of it. I want to protect you from everything that Satan offers you and through which he wants to destroy you. As I bore Jesus in my womb, so also, dear children, do I wish to bear you unto holiness. God wants to save you and sends you messages through men, nature, and so many things, which can only help you to understand that you must change the direction of your life. Therefore, little children, understand also the greatness of the gift which God is giving you through me, so that I may protect you with my mantle and lead you to the joy of life. Thank you for having responded to my call.

Franciscan University Press
Franciscan University
Steubenville, OH 43952 U.S.A.

ISBN 0-940535-31-9

Međugorje Publishing Group
MEĐUGORJE TODAY
© 1990 by
Sonnenhaus Verlag Jelenko Rastić
D-7416 Trochtelfingen

ISBN 3-924902-03-8

Tomislav Rastić
Horvatovac 15
YU-41000 Zagreb

ISBN 86-81443-04-6

Photographs
Tomislav Rastić
(2, 4/5, 6, 8, 12/13, 15, 19, 20, 23, 38, 40, 41, 43, 44,
45, 46, 48/49, 50, 51, 52, 56, 58/59, 60, 63, 68/69, 71,
72, 73, 76, 77, 80, 81, 84, 85, 94, 120, 121, cover)
Tomaž Lauko
(11, 16, 17, 18, 24, 25, 28, 30, 31, 32, 33, 34, 35, 36, 37)
Zlata Vucelić
(66, 88, 89, 90, 100, 101, 106, 107, 108, 109, 112, 113)
Jelenko Rastić
(42, 47, 54, 55, 126/127)

Editor
Jelenko Rastić

Art Director
Tomislav Rastić

Translated by
Volga & Tony Dawe, Zagreb

Reviewed by
Dr Viktor Nuić, OFM
Branimir Donat

Printed in Yugoslavia by Gorenjski tisk, Kranj